STO

12/18/07

ALLEN COUNTY PUBLIC LIBRARY

ACPL IT

DISCARDED

S0-BXC-596

REALITY
MILLIONAIRE
Proven Tips
to Retire Rich

MIKE PETERSON

Reality Media, Inc.

Reality Millionaire—Proven Tips to Retire Rich
Copyright © 2007 Reality Media, Inc.
Published by Reality Media, Inc.

All rights reserved. No part of this book may be reproduced (except for inclusion in reviews), disseminated or utilized in any form or by any means, electronic or mechanical, including photocopying, recording, or in any information storage and retrieval system, or the Internet/World Wide Web without written permission from the author or publisher.

This publication is designed to provide accurate and authoritative information in regard to the subject matter covered. It is sold with the understanding that neither the author nor the publisher is engaged in rendering financial, accounting, legal, or other professional services by publishing this book. If financial advice or other expert assistance is needed, the service of a competent professional should be sought. The author and publisher specifically disclaim any liability, loss or risk resulting from the use or application of the information contained in this book.

Visit our Web site at:
www.realitymillionaire.com

Reality Millionaire is a trademark of Reality Media, Inc.

BOOK DESIGN BY
ARBOR BOOKS, INC.
19 SPEAR ROAD, SUITE 301
RAMSEY, NJ 07446

PRINTED IN THE UNITED STATES

MIKE PETERSON
REALITY MILLIONAIRE—PROVEN TIPS TO RETIRE RICH

1. AUTHOR 2. TITLE 3. PERSONAL FINANCE/ FINANCIAL PLANNING/ MONEY MANAGEMENT

LIBRARY OF CONGRESS CONTROL NUMBER: 2006936546
ISBN 10: 0-9768185-1-5
ISBN 13: 978-0-9768185-1-9

Dedication

"This book is dedicated to all those who truly seek financial freedom."

TABLE OF CONTENTS

Establish your life goals and figure out how much they
might cost.

Learn how to free up 10% to 15% of your income
and start building an emergency fund.

A few simple tips to thinking about your finances in a
different light.

REALITY MILLIONAIRE

PROVEN TIPS TO RETIRE RICH

How would you like to play the latest and greatest reality game? Would you sign up if I told you the payout was **one million dollars?** How about if the only competition you faced was yourself? You don't have to live out in the wilderness for 30 days. No hunting for your own food. You don't need to do anything life threatening, or heaven forbid, eat something that would make a cockroach blanch. There's no chance that you might not receive the coveted rose, and you're guaranteed to win if you follow the rules.

What if I told you there were **just nine rounds?** And that winning these nine rounds was something anybody could do with minimal effort and only a few small commitments? What if you knew that even "cheating" a time or two would not disqualify you, and that all the factors of the game are largely under your control? Would you want to play?

My guess is that you would jump at the chance to play this game and take home a million bucks. Who wouldn't? Imagine the freedom that $1,000,000 would give you. What an exciting challenge this game must be! What a rush it would be to win!

What if I told you that this game has been around since the beginning of time? And that everyone in the world plays this game on a daily basis? It's an exciting game for some, and for others it is the bane of their existence. Most people dream of winning the game, yet very few are actually prepared to play.

What if I told you, you were already playing the game, and that you are probably losing?

My name is Mike Peterson and 15 years ago, I was thousands of dollars in debt. I'd made some bad decisions and lost my life's savings on a start-up I'd created with some of my friends. Every credit card was maxed, I had zero assets, and when I went to the bank to get a loan to start a new business, they told me my income was too low for my debt.

"But I need the money to get out of debt," I said.

"That's not our problem," they said.

Sound familiar? We spend years and thousands of dollars in school learning about math, English, history and science. We learn trades. We get out in the world and we make money. But no one ever taught us how to manage that money. Did we all miss the class on financial freedom?

For many of us, financial management skills aren't passed down from our parents or from our teachers. Why? Truth is, many of them don't know how to manage their money either. How are any of us supposed to get rich if none of us knows how to get from financial A to Z? We can't. And the fact is, getting from financial A to Z is so easy that anyone with any level of education can do it. It doesn't take a Master's in Accounting, and you don't have to be an investment genius.

Despite the fact that anyone can become a millionaire, the vast majority of Americans never stop to learn the simple rules of financial management that will lead them there. As a co-founder of a nonprofit consumer credit counseling organization, I saw people every day that would shy away from doing their finances. Most of them will work hard 40 hours a week to make money, but won't spend one hour of that week managing it. It's my belief that they don't really understand how much of a difference it can make in their lives. I think most people really don't understand that they could come out of the game a real-life Reality Millionaire. If they did, wouldn't everybody be doing it?

I know you're skeptical, but it's true: Everyone (and I mean everyone) can be a Reality Millionaire. How do I know? I've been there firsthand, and today, 15 years from being thousands of dollars in debt, I have over one million dollars in assets, investments and cash. My house and cars are paid off. My debt is paid off. My credit card balances are zero.

Did I win in Vegas? No. Do I make seven figures a year? Not a chance. I learned how to play the game. I learned how to play Reality Millionaire, work with the numbers I had, and come out a winner. These steps have worked so well for me that I have spent the last seven years teaching them to others. There is no reason why everyone can't have enough for retirement or for their life's dreams.

You can do it too. In a world where personal debt is at its highest levels, where a staggering percent of divorce is caused by money troubles, and where the average American spends $1.22 for every $1.00 that he makes, there is a way out of the downward financial spiral.

In fact, I have a promise for you: I promise you that whatever your finances look like now, you can play Reality Millionaire and win. I promise you that anyone on any income can get out of debt and enjoy new levels of financial freedom by playing just nine rounds of this life-changing game. I promise you that you can do this without giving up all your worldly pleasures. You can do it using money you currently have—money that exists in your current finances that you don't even know you have.

You might even find that it's fun. After all, who doesn't like to win the game?

But before you start to play, you have to make a simple commitment. You have to make a small promise to yourself. You have to understand that only you can take control of your finances—that although outside events can happen (heaven knows, bad luck happens to everyone), you can't blame outside sources for your financial troubles

THE COMMITMENT

I will play Reality Millionaire for at least twelve months, and during these months, I will do my best to follow the rules of Reality Millionaire. I understand that only I have the power to change my financial situation, and I am ready to commit to making a change in my life to do so. I understand that, as in any game, there may be setbacks and roadblocks, but I will overcome these and continue playing. I do this because I believe it will make me a happier, more well rounded person and more importantly because . . .

I WANT TO BE A MILLIONAIRE

Signed_____ Date_____

MEET JOE AND JANE AVERAGE

Let me introduce you to the Average Family. Joe and Jane Average just happen to be average in every way. They each have average jobs, they make an average income, and they have average debts. They live in an average home in a city whose financial demographics are the exact average of all cities across the United States.

Joe and Jane are going to help us out with some of our examples in Reality Millionaire. I know nobody is truly average, but I'll need to use some average figures to show you how to play the game. (Yes, I did say figures. Don't wince. You don't have to be a math whiz to figure them out—I promise.) And don't worry. Just because you don't fit Joe and Jane's figures exactly, it doesn't mean you can't play the game. Anyone can play, and anyone can win.

Name: Joe and Jane Average

Family Income: $44,389
Mortgage: $136,000
Car Loans: $23,000
Other Loans: $3,300
Credit Cards: $8,400

Bank Balance: Zero.

Family Description: Hate to budget. Dream of becoming millionaires, but have no firm game plan to do so. Live paycheck to paycheck. Cover debts, but feel weighed down by them.

They work hard, but never get ahead.

Are you ready? Lets play Round One. . . .

ROUND ONE

Defining Your Finish Line

Wisdom is to live in the present, plan for the future and profit from the past. —Anonymous

If you're like most people in America, you suffer from a few common bad habits concerning your money mindset. Chances are you have big dreams but no big plans.

You may want to get a bigger house someday, or you want to have enough money to buy a timeshare at your favorite ski resort. You and your spouse may plan to do a tour of Europe after the kids leave. Your lifetime dream may be to take up sailing or golf or furnish that game room in the den. Then of course, there are other things you'll need to pay for throughout your lifetime: your children's education, your car payments, your roof repairs. . . .

Of course, you don't have any idea how you're going to pay for any of this. You figure, if you just keep on truckin', the money will just sort of happen. But for most of us, money doesn't just happen. The sad fact is that most of us end up at the finish line of the big game in worse shape than we started: in debt, out of money and with most of our big dreams unfulfilled.

You see, most of us don't understand how much life costs. In the first round of Reality Millionaire, we need to take a closer look at how much money you need to pay for the goals that you have. We need to define your finish line, so you know where to go to win the game.

For example, here are a few things you may want to do with your life

Goals	Estimated Cost
Vacation once a year for 20 years.	$60,000
Purchase a vacation home.	$150,000
Pay for your children's education.	$60,000
Buy a bigger house.	$300,000
Pay for your daughter's wedding.	$10,000
Be a millionaire	$1,000,000
TOTAL	**$1.58 Million**

How much does all this cost? *Over one and a half million dollars!* And that doesn't include your living costs for the next 20 years. It also doesn't account for the three new cars you'll probably need to buy before retirement, or the plumbing and foundation repairs on your house, or Christmas, or birthdays, or teenagers.

Well, it's probably not as bad as it seems. After all, you make an income, right? Maybe if you added it all up, you'd come up with a big enough number to pay for all of your big goals.

Now, I don't know what your income is, but I do know that the Median Family Income in 2005 was $44,389 per year. If you add up all of the money the average family will make in the next 30 years, you come up with $1.3 million.

Notice a discrepancy? How on earth is an average Joe supposed to make enough money to support his family, keep food on the table and a roof over their heads, and still save enough money to pay for all the fun things in life? And of course, everybody wants to be a millionaire. Maybe it's just not possible. Maybe the entire American Dream is just one big farce, and there really is no way for regular people to make that much money.

But maybe your numbers are better. Let's see how your numbers add up. Insert some Life Goals in the left hand column and their estimated costs in the right. You don't have to be too specific; we're just getting some averages here.

Goals	Estimated Cost
Be a millionaire	$1,000,000
TOTAL	

Now multiply your current income times 30 to get your Thirty Year Income and insert the number here: _____.

How are your numbers looking?

If you're like the vast majority of people out there, the numbers aren't looking very good. In fact, you probably didn't even list half of what you'd like to do in your lifetime, and your total income is still less than it will take to pay for your lifetime dreams. Are we all just fooling ourselves? Should we give up hope now?

After playing Round One of Reality Millionaire, you've lined up your goals, but chances are you're feeling worse than ever. There is simply no way you can come up with that much money. Right now you're probably thinking about giving up the whole game.

But, luckily for you, you signed The Commitment back on Page 4. So you've got to at least take a peek at Round Two. After all, I promised you anyone could enjoy financial freedom, so there must be some way out of this dilemma. Don't worry—there is!

To Recap:

- Most people have big dreams, but never think about how to fund them.

- It's important to understand how much money you'll need in your lifetime to accomplish the things you want.

- It's important to understand how much money you'll be making over the next decades on your current income.

- If you need more money for your life dreams than you could ever make in a lifetime, you are in the same boat as almost everybody.

- You can still achieve your life dreams, even though the numbers don't seem to add up.

- You can do this by learning how to manage your money, which I will show you in the following rounds of Reality Millionaire.

3 1833 05336 6743

ROUND TWO

Beware of little expenses: a small leak will sink
a great ship. —Ben Franklin (1706–1790)

What if I told you that you could "find" extra money in your current situation, amounting to between 10% and 15% of your income—and that you could find this money without sacrificing anything that you love, without working an extra job, and without winning the lottery? You might think, "No way. Not me. Other people who make more have extra money, but not with my budget."

I see people everyday who are absolutely miserable because they don't make "enough money." What might shock you is that when you look at their incomes, they range from as little as $20,000 per year up to as much as $250,000 per year, yet they all have the same problem: Not enough money.

How on earth could anyone making $250,000 a year have money troubles? The one thing that all of these people have in common is that they never learned how to manage their money. The bottom line is that it really doesn't matter how much you make. It's what you do with it that determines financial freedom or frustration.

I've been teaching classes in financial management for years, and I have never met anyone that couldn't find this extra money in their current budget. And they don't have to eat bread and water every night to find it, either.

The first thing that you have to do to find this extra money is to look at your expenses. Sit down with a pen and paper and write it down: mortgage payment, electric bill, phone bill, cable bill, everything.

Write down all the monthly expenses you can think of and chances are you're still staring at your list and scratching your head. Don't feel bad. The average American family cannot account for **10% to 15% of their income.** Don't believe me? Try it. When Joe and Jane Average tried it, they came up with the expense list on the right. Try inserting yours on the left.

Your Expenses

_____
_____
_____
_____
_____
_____
_____
_____
_____
_____
_____
_____

Your Income: _____

**Do your expenses
match your income?**

When the Average Family wrote down their expenses, their first attempt looked something like this . . .

Joe and Jane's Expense List

Mortgage:	$895
Phone:	$55
Utilities:	$180
Water:	$30
TV/Cable:	$60
Internet:	$30
Credit Cards:	$215
Auto Loan and Insurance:	$315
Other Loans:	$130
Groceries:	$270

Total Expenses: $2180

Joe and Jane Average make $3699 per month. Obviously, they're missing something. Where is the rest of it going?

Chances are you're not sure where all the money is going. For that you'll need a . . .

BIGGER PIECE OF PAPER
Here's One to Get You Started

Your Expenses	
Home Rent or Mortgage Home Insurance Home Maintenance Property Taxes	**Children & Education** Educational Loans Daycare or Private School School Supplies School Fees Baby Supplies Allowance
Utilities Electricity Telephone Water Garbage Pickup Homeowner/Condo Fees Internet Connection Natural Gas Cable TV	**Entertainment** Renting or Going to Movies Family Outings Entertaining Tobacco Alcohol Vacations
Food Groceries Dining Out Take Out	**Pets** Pet Grooming Pet Boarding Pet Medical Pet Food
Transportation Car Loan Car insurance Gas Parking Car Maintenance & Repairs Subway, Tolls & Bus Registration & Inspection	**Services** Housekeeper Gardner/Mower Babysitter
Personal Care Hair Cuts Manicures/Pedicures Dry Cleaning Gym Memberships	**Medical** Dentist Physician Eye Care Prescriptions Emergencies Medical Insurance Life & Disability Insurance

Consumer Items	Other Expenses
Magazines & Subscriptions	Other Loans
Club Memberships	Credit Card Payments
Books	
Hobby Expenses	**Child Support**
DVDs & CDs	Late Fees, Bank
Clothes	Charges, etc.
Furniture/Household	Charity
Computers & Home	Alimony
Office	Income Tax
Toys & Games	
Gifts	**Savings**
Christmas Expenditures	Retirement Savings
Other	Emergency Savings
	Investments

You probably don't have solid figures for a lot of these categories. Few people actually keep track of what they spend on movie rentals, haircuts, parking, or pets, but all those little expenses add up.

To get some more concrete numbers, **track your expenses for at least seven days.** This sounds like a superfluous step, but it's not. In fact, if you can track your expenses for at least 30 days, you'll get a much better estimate. And it's an absolutely essential part to playing Reality Millionaire. So don't cheat! Track your expenses every time you find yourself in front of a cash register a vending machine, a tollbooth, a checkbook, or an ATM machine. Every time you use that spare change to buy your six-year-old a gumball, write it down.

In your first day of tracking, you'll probably notice some interesting things are happening.

Perhaps you realized that on your way to work everyday you buy yourself a bottle of water and a donut. Or that each day, you spend $10 eating lunch at a restaurant. Maybe you buy a snack from the company vending machine every evening that costs you a dollar.

When you sit down at the end of the week, you'll most likely discover that you are spending an awful lot of money on some things that you really don't need.

MORE SAVING TIPS

- Buy generic
- Use dishcloths, not paper towels
- Save ketchup from drive-thru's
- Eat at home
- Rent movies instead of going to the theater
- Avoid impulse items at the convenience store
- Quit something (smoking, lottery tickets, chocolate)
- Use a clothesline instead of a dryer

- Do it yourself when it comes to home projects
- Make your own Christmas gifts *(needlework, cookies, etc.)*
- Order water at restaurants
- Don't let sales lure you into buying items you wouldn't normally buy.
- Buy wrapping paper after Christmas and save it for next year.

- Buy swimsuits in December and coats in July.
- Buy used clothes.
- Refinance every time you can save money on the deal.
- Turn off the lights in rooms you aren't using.
- Shop at "Scratch & Dent" or Clearance Stores
- Turn off extra electrical appliances.

In fact, the average person can save about a hundred dollars a month if they just cut down on a couple of very small things. For example, that donut and bottled water that costs $3.50 a day? That costs $105 a month. So bring your own water to work and forget the donut. Wasn't that easy?

Do you pay for lunch everyday? Brown-bag it and save another $50 or $60, even with the cost of lunch meat and sandwich bread. Of course, you don't want to give up all of your daily indulgences. But, when you do the math, chances are about 15% of your income is going to very small, frivolous expenses that you don't really need.

The trick is to find a good balance between being responsible and giving yourself a few treats now and then. Most people find that balance at around 10% of their income, or $370 for the average Joe. That's right. The average family can save as much as $370 a month by just cutting down on a few impulse buys.

OK, fine, you might say. I might be able to find some extra income here and there, but how do I turn a few hundred dollars a month into over a million dollars? For that, you will need to proceed to Round Three.

BUT FIRST, you need to use that $370 for something REALLY important. I know, I know, you are anxious to get on to making the big bucks. But before we do that, there is a major step we need to take to set the stage for your money-making adventure. You need a safety net.

They say, "don't count your chickens before they hatch" because you never know what is going to happen, right? Well, since you never know what is going to happen, you have to be prepared for anything and everything: you lose your job, you get in an accident and can't work, a hurricane destroys your house . . . you don't want to think about it, but emergencies do happen. Ease the fear and worry by saving up for a rainy day so you can weather the storm.

Go to www.realitymillionaire.com, if you want to make this step easier, and request the FREE booklet "Debt-Free in Record Time" It is a small workbook that will help you track your expenses, find the "savings," build an emergency fund, and start a debt elimination plan. It's a totally free booklet provided by my friends at the American Credit Foundation®.

BUILDING AN EMERGENCY FUND

You know all that extra money we just found in your income? This is where it's going to come in handy.

Approximately half of all Americans live paycheck to paycheck, meaning many of us are just one paycheck away from homelessness.

You may be excited to jump the gun and rush headlong into Round Three to start making the big bucks. But you can't. Why not? Because if you're like most of us, you haven't built up an Emergency Fund. You probably don't like to think about getting ill or the car breaking down or the kids getting a parking ticket. You don't even like to think about little emergencies, like the vet bill after your cat Freddy's tail got slammed in the garage door.

Reality is—and you are playing Reality Millionaire—unexpected expenses happen. Your plumbing gets backed up and gunk fills up your bathtub, your meter runs out and you get a parking ticket, or your back windshield gets busted out when you stop in for a burger on the wrong side of town. How will you pay for all that if you don't build an Emergency Fund? You'd have to borrow, finance or pay with a credit card—all lousy options as we'll discover in later rounds.

To avoid whipping out the credit cards, you have to learn how to play things smart. You must use that money that you made by cutting expenses earlier in Round Two and put it into an Emergency Fund. I know, boring, right? Don't worry, we'll get to do something fun with it after you finish this part. But for now, play by the rules, and save it for a rainy day.

An Emergency Fund should cover at least three months of base living expenses, meaning that you could live for three months off of your Emergency Fund without losing your home, your car, or your electricity while still covering your base needs.

You may have a few setbacks along the way. After all, during the time you're saving for emergencies, you're likely to have a couple. You may have to withdraw some money for an unexpected dentist bill or a new bumper after a fender bender, but don't give up.

If you run into an emergency while you're saving for your Emergency Fund, and you don't have enough money to cover it, find it. Have a garage sale. Count your loose change. Have your kids pitch in and put up a lemonade stand. Your friends might have some odd jobs you could do: gardening, paperwork, answering phones at the office.

Depending on your unique situation, it will probably take you between six months and two years to fully fund your Emergency Fund. But hang in there. It will pay off in the end.

When you have three months of living expenses saved up, you'll feel pretty accomplished. If you've never had an Emergency Fund before, this may be the most cash you've ever saved. If you used to have enough to feel comfortable, now you do again.

After building your Emergency Fund you have reached the first, most basic level of security—the security of not having to live one month away from poverty. If worse comes to worse, you know you and your family will have three months to get back on your feet.

Now you are ready to move on to Round Three. Weeeeelllll . . . almost.

To Recap:

- You have extra money in your current budget that you don't realize you have.

- Chances are you will not be able to account for 10% to 15% of your expenditures on your first try.

- Most of this money is going towards unnecessary expenses.

- Without giving up anything you will miss, you can easily save at least 10% of your income.

- Part of being a wise, sensible Reality Millionaire is creating an Emergency Fund.

- This fund will gain you the first level of security: the security of knowing that you and your family will be OK for at least three months if your income completely stops.

- To create this fund, deposit the "extra" money you found at the beginning of Round Two into a savings account until you save up three months of living expenses.

But First . . .

ROUND TWO POINT FIVE

A FEW TIPS TO HELP YOU
CHANGE YOUR MONEY MINDSET

Never spend your money before you have it. —Thomas Jefferson

Did I say nine rounds of Reality Millionaire? So I fibbed a little. Let's call it nine and a half. Most of Round 2.5 isn't so much a step as a frame of mind. To succeed at Reality Millionaire you will have to change your money mindset. You have to learn a few simple rules by which we play the game

Rule #1: Think in Years, Not Months.

You probably like to think of your budget (when you think of it at all) in terms of months. You make X amount per month, therefore you can spend X amount per month.

So, when you think about what you can afford, you think in terms of payments and sales prices, but not what things will cost you once you've finished with 30 or 60 or 90 or 1000 monthly payments. To win Reality Millionaire, you have to start thinking about your income and expenses over the long haul. Why is that so important? Because . . .

Rule #2: Paying Interest is *Bad*.

Let me give you an example: You decide to buy a stereo. You scour the sales, read the consumer reports, even visit several stores. You find the best deal on a system you know you're going to love.

You can't believe the bargain you've found! The $4,000 system you want is reduced a full grand, and you can put it on the store credit card for a minimum payment starting at only $60.00 a month. You don't like to think in years, so you never bother to figure out how much that stereo will actually cost you. Out comes the credit card and home goes the stereo system. No big deal, right?

Now let's see what that stereo system is actually costing you. Paying the monthly minimum, at 18% interest—not bad for store credit—you would pay over $7,900 in interest over the next 37 years. That's a total of over $10,900 for that $3,000 stereo system. Of course, by that time, you would have needed several new stereo systems, which you would also be paying for.

Well, who cares, right? So you pay a ton more, but that's what credit is all about. You pay them extra money so you don't have to pay all of that money upfront. But did you ever think about what else you could do with that money? That is, did you ever think about what that money could do for you if you were making interest on it instead of paying interest with it?

Those minimum payments every month may not seem like much, but if you took the money you spent on interest and spent it in investments instead, you could easily have made over $12,000 during the time you paid out well over $7,000!

So how do you avoid paying interest? By following . . .

Rule #3: Control the Consumer in You.

Learn to distinguish between wants and needs. Cutting a little bit here and there can make a big difference to the amount of financial freedom you are able to enjoy. You need the milk on your grocery list. You want the People Magazine in the impulse aisle. You need to pay the phone bill. You want call waiting and caller ID and voice-mail. Does that mean you should turn off your caller ID and that you can't ever buy a magazine from the checkout aisle? No. What it means is that it's important to recognize those things for what they are: small luxuries. Enjoy your small luxuries, but deny yourself every once in a while as well. It will make an amazing difference to the bottom line—to the amount of money you have for big purchases at the end of every year. And you'll appreciate your small luxuries that much more when you indulge.

There's another bad habit that most of us have when making purchases, and that's the natural human tendency to be optimistic. Yes! In this, even pessimists are optimistic. We all think we'll have more money tomorrow than we have today. Which leads us to . . .

Rule #4: Don't Count Your Chickens Before They Hatch.

It's one of the most common (and the worst) money managing habits out there: buying things based on future income—and salesmen bend over backwards trying to get you to do it. How many promotions have you seen in the last month: 0 down, 0% financing until next year. What's your impulse? "Sounds great! Buy now. Pay later. What could possibly go wrong?"

Well, there are, of course, the catastrophes: you lose your job, you become ill, or your house burns down; but barring those, there are still plenty of reasons you should think twice about taking advantage of one of those deals.

Putting off payments is not necessarily a good thing. It just means that you're doubling up on payments later. After all, if you wait until next Christmas to start paying off stuff that you buy this Christmas, does that mean you're going to skip Christmas next year? No. You'll buy more stuff next Christmas and your payments will start piling up. Pretty soon you'll find that your debt is out of control, and trust me, when you're still paying for that entertainment system you bought five years ago, those pure tones that the salesman raved about won't sound so sweet.

Here's another common scenario . . . "The Promotion You're **Sure** About."

You've been promised a promotion in January, so you decide to celebrate with a hip new ride. But all the sales on this year's models are in December, and you don't want to miss out. The Lexus dealership is offering $0 down and 0% interest for six months. The payments are a little bit more than you can really afford on this year's salary, but after the promotion and the fat pay raise, you won't have any problems with them at all. Right?

What happens? The office upstart gets the promotion instead, leaving you no choice but to trade in your new car for an older model when the payments come due. To make matters worse, when you go to trade it in, you discover that you're upside-down on the car (having never made a payment, but having put plenty of miles on it), and you've got to shell out a couple of grand just to get rid of the thing. Why didn't anyone tell you that your car would lose 20% of its resale value in the first year?

The moral of the story is: you can have hope and positive expectations, but you cannot risk making assumptions about things you simply aren't sure of, especially when it comes to your finances.

Rule #5: Being Wealthy is About What You Save, Not What You Have.

It's a natural tendency to want to appear wealthier than you are. But what most people don't realize is that being wealthy is about what's in the bank, not about how much stuff you have. A fancy car and a big stereo system may make you look wealthy, but when your bank balance is zero, you're actually one step away from poverty.

What's the definition of rich? Is it having a big house? No. It's having money, which means cash. If you are always maxing out your monthly living expenses trying to appear rich, then you'll always be nothing more than a member of the economy assembly line— working, making money, and passing it down, without ever keeping any for yourself. And what do you get at the end of the road? A big fat zero in the bank account, and a big fat F in Reality Millionaire.

To Recap:

- To succeed at Reality Millionaire, you have to change the way you handle your money in day-to-day situations.

- When you think about how much things are costing, add them up in cost per year or cost per decade, not cost per month.

- More of your money goes to interest than you realize. Paying interest is the number one reason most Americans will never become financially successful.

- Learning to distinguish needs from wants and avoiding impulse purchases will go a long way towards helping you save enough money to meet your Life Goals.

- Never purchase based on future income.

- In order to be wealthy, you must have money in the bank or in investments. Simply appearing wealthy does not make one wealthy.

ROUND THREE

GET BACK TO THE STARTING LINE

A bird in the hand is worth two in the bush. —*Latin Proverb*

Before you can win the game, you have to get back to the starting block. You see, so far you have been running the race backward. Instead of saving money, you've been borrowing money. You need to get back to ground zero, so you can stop paying interest, and start making interest.

For that you need to learn the most important rule of all:

**The Golden Rule of
Reality Millionaire**
**Never charge more than
you can pay back on your
next statement.**

Sound impossible? It's not. Instead of paying backward, start paying it forward. What does that mean? If you want a $3,000 stereo system, practice Controlling the Consumer in You and settle for a $1,000 system instead. Then, instead of charging the system and paying for it retroactively, save a few hundred dollars towards it every month—pay it forward. When you have enough money saved, pay for the system in full. Trust me, you'll feel a lot better about rewarding yourself, and it will make a huge difference to the amount of money you end up with at the end of the game.

And remember, *paying interest is bad.* When you make only the minimum payments, you will pay approximately **four times the cost** of the merchandise by the time it is paid off. When you follow The Golden Rule, you only pay the actual cost of what you buy.

In fact, The Golden Rule is so very important that I will say: If you can't follow this rule, you can't win the game. Period. So never cheat on this one. Ever.

Once you promise to follow The Golden Rule, the next step to getting back to the starting line is to create a Debt Elimination Plan. It's easy (much easier than following The Golden Rule). All you have to do is follow two simple steps.

CREATING A DEBT ELIMINATION PLAN

Step One. Determine How Much You Owe.

Separate out all of your debts from the list of expenses you made in Round Two. List each creditor first and the total amount required to pay off each debt. Then add up each debt and arrive at the total. This is the total amount you will have to repay to get back to the starting line.

When Joe and Jane Average tried it, they came up with the debt list on the right. Try inserting yours on the left.

Your Total Debt

Creditor	Total Owed
_____	_____
_____	_____
_____	_____
_____	_____
_____	_____
_____	_____
_____	_____
_____	_____
_____	_____

Your Total Debt: _____

When the Average Family wrote their debts down, their list looked something like this:

Joe and Jane Average's Total Debt

Mortgage:	$136,000
Car Loans:	$12,000
Other Loans:	$3,300
Credit Cards:	$8,400

Total Debt: $159,700

Chances are about now you're wondering how you ever got into such a hole. How will you ever repay it? It seems impossible. Don't worry. It's not as bad as it looks.

You are repaying your debt slowly, through monthly payments. After all, the whole reason you borrowed all that money in the first place was because you weren't keeping hundreds of thousands of dollars lying around in cold hard cash. The trick is to learn how to speed up those payments and get out of debt sooner—without breaking the bank.

To do that, we first need to learn how much you owe your creditors every month. Insert your monthly debt payments in the list to the left.

Your Monthly Debt Payment

Creditor	Payment
_____	_____
_____	_____
_____	_____
_____	_____
_____	_____
_____	_____
_____	_____
_____	_____

Your Total Debt Payment: _____

Joe and Jane's Monthly Payment List

Car Payment:	$243
Credit Cards:	
Visa	$125
MasterCard	$75
AMEX	$15
Personal Loan:	$130
Home Loan:	$895

Total Monthly Payments: $1483

In the United States, the average total family debt payment is about $1483 per month. Added to the average amount of "extra" money the typical family can find in their current budget from Round Two, that's about $1850 extra the average family could put in their pocket every month if they didn't owe anybody else any money.

Of course, your numbers will differ from this, but chances are your numbers are just as astounding. Think about what you could do with $1,000 or $2,000 or $5,000 extra every month! The possibilities are exciting. But the average family (with a mortgage and a car loan) also owes over $159,000 in debt, and if they stick to paying their current monthly minimums it will take them 25 to 35 years to pay it all off! Chances are that that is pretty much the rest of their working lifetime.

INTERESTING FACT: The Federal Reserve Bank of Cleveland reports that the debt-to-income ratio has nearly doubled over the last two decades, while the personal savings rate in the U.S. has declined nearly 10%.

Are we all destined to spend the rest of our lives paying other people off? What good is it to pay off all our your debts and get back to the starting line if you're ready for the old-folks home by the time you get it all paid back? You want to earn your financial freedom in time to enjoy it.

There is a way. You must eliminate the words "monthly minimum" from your vocabulary and commit yourself today to a fixed monthly payment. Don't worry. It won't be any more money then you're spending now. Here's how . . .

Step Two. Commit Yourself to a Fixed Monthly Payment

Promise yourself that you will always pay at least the minimum monthly payment that you came up with when you added up all of your debts. Even as the minimum required monthly payments decrease, you will continue to pay at least this amount every month towards your Debt Elimination Plan. As you pay off your first debts, you will use the monthly payment that you were making against that debt to put extra money into payments on your other debts. This is called "rolling your payments over."

Here's an example using Joe and Jane Average's numbers. Joe and Jane Average's total debt payment is $1483. Therefore they must commit to pay at least $1483 every month towards their Debt Elimination Plan, even when their minimum monthly payments start to go down. Once they pay off their first debt (let's say a MasterCard balance), they will use the money they were paying to the MasterCard to pay towards another creditor. They will probably choose to pay it to the creditor with the highest interest rate.

In addition to paying at least the fixed monthly payment you calculated, you must also always follow The Golden Rule and pay off everything you charged that month. So, even in the month of December, when you're tempted to use those cards to buy the newest plasma screen TV and digital camera, you will not buy anything that you don't already have the money for.

Your **total monthly payment every month** will always be the fixed monthly payment you calculated for your Debt Elimination Plan PLUS whatever you charged that month. Making this payment and following this step is essential to winning Reality Millionaire.

But what if you think you can pay off this month's credit card charges in just two months? Surely, you think, that wouldn't be so bad. **Don't do it!** The Golden Rule is crucial to Reality Millionaire. Think of it like an exercise schedule: Skipping one week and going back to it the next week is agony, but when you do it routinely, you won't find it hard at all. And just like exercising, following The Golden Rule and adhering to your Debt Elimination Plan will give you peace of mind and will lower your stress level.

But will paying these fixed payments to your Debt Elimination Plan really make that much of a difference in the end? When you look at your statements, you probably feel overwhelmed. It's going to take forever to pay them all off anyway—it almost seems worth it to revert to paying the minimums.

But it will make a huge difference. Here's a mini-example using the Average Family's credit card balance.

> Joe and Jane's current credit card balance is $8,400. Their credit card is at 18.9% interest.
>
> Their minimum monthly payment today for their credit card is $215.
>
> **Using a Fixed Payment**
> If the Averages use their Debt Elimination Plan, and pay today's minimum monthly payment of $215 each month, and they continue to pay $215 even as the minimum payments start to decrease, it will take them **60 months** (5 years) and cost them **$4,400.79 in interest** to pay off their credit card debt.

> **Paying the Minimum**
>
> The amount of interest they are paying using the Debt Elimination Plan may seem like a lot—until you look at the alternative. If the Averages pay only the minimum each month, it will take them **252 months** (21 years) and they will pay **$11,181.42 in interest** before they pay off their $8400.00 credit card debt!

Applying this simple Debt Elimination Plan to their total debt, the average American family can get out of debt in about 13 years (instead of well over 30) and they will save more than $100,000 in interest!

Play With Your Own Numbers

Still having a little trouble visualizing exactly how much money you can save when you make a monthly fixed credit card payment? The truth about credit card interest packs a bigger punch when you can see how it works with your own numbers. Check out our Credit Card Calculator at www.realitymillionaire.com, and see how much money you can save with this simple Debt Elimination Plan.

To Recap:

- To win Reality Millionaire, you have to get back to the starting line—stop paying interest and become debt free.

- To do this, you must first commit to The Golden Rule of Reality Millionaire: Never Charge More Than You Can Pay Back on Your Next Statement.

- Next, you must formulate a Debt Elimination Plan.

- First write down all of your debts and add up your minimum monthly payment.

- Second, commit to paying that minimum monthly payment as a minimum fixed payment until all of your debts are paid off.

- Combining The Golden Rule with your Debt Elimination Plan, your total monthly payment every month will always be the fixed monthly payment you calculated PLUS whatever you charged that month.

- Applying your Debt Elimination Plan will get you out of the hole, back at the starting line, and on the right track to winning Reality Millionaire.

ROUND FOUR

*A LITTLE FORTUNE TELLING
AND THE POWER OF INVESTMENT*

*The most powerful force in the universe is compound
interest. —Albert Einstein*

After saving up your Emergency Fund, and starting to pay down
your debts, you are feeling a little better about your finances, but
you're probably still skeptical about this Reality Millionaire thing.
After all, a few thousand dollars in an Emergency Fund is a long
haul from becoming a millionaire. And when we added up our Life
Goals, we already determined that just saving money isn't going to
be enough. We could squirrel money away under a pillow for years
and still not make a million. So, where is this extraordinary wealth
going to come from?

*Your million dollars will come by making use
of the one trick that all millionaires
understand and use everyday:
They make money off of their money.*

You're probably thinking, Yeah, sure. That only works for millionaires, but I don't have enough money to do that. I've only got a measly few hundred dollars a month. Big deal. But it is a big deal. Your measly few hundred dollars a month can turn into hundreds of thousands of dollars. No scams. No shams. Just sound money management.

In Round Four, I'm going to teach you how to be a bit of a fortune-teller. We're going to learn what the **Power of Investment** can do for you, and we're going to look into your future 20 years down the road and see in real numbers how your finances will flourish.

Now let's get some FREE money!

What if I told you that in 10 years, you could receive a $10,000 check. And you wouldn't have to do anything to earn it—that it would be completely free money. You wouldn't have to work one extra day, or even one extra hour. Wouldn't you want it? Would you say no?

Ten years from now, by investing only $370 a month, you can easily make an extra $10,000 or $20,000 or even $50,000, not counting your original investments. It's time to start taking advantage of the free money that banks and financial institutions are offering you.

You'll start learning about investing by using the extra money you found from Round Two that you first used to build your Emergency Fund. At first, your investments may not seem to add up to very much. After all, every month the average American family can only find $370 extra dollars in their budget. And you're sure that Daddy Warbucks and Donald Trump didn't make their millions investing $370 a month. But then you remember that as soon as you fully complete your Debt Elimination Plan, you will have thousands extra each month to put towards investments (around $1,850 if you're the Average Joe). Now that's some serious money.

But investing sounds scary. After all, you aren't a stockbroker or a financial analyst. Isn't just saving money safer? You don't want to lose it. Don't worry. There are plenty of safe ways to earn a return on your money (and plenty of riskier ways for those who enjoy a walk on the wild side). Whether you like to play it safe or not, there are simple steps to investing that will take the mystery out of the World of Finance.

Who Says Money Doesn't Grow on Trees?

The Two Big Ways To Make FREE Money.

When you earn money on your money, that is called a **Return on Investment,** or ROI. There are many ways to generate an ROI, but they basically fall into two categories:

1. Loan your money to someone who wants it and who **will pay you interest** to use it. You make interest from things like savings accounts or treasury bonds.

2. Purchase something that you believe **will increase in value** over the time that you own it. This is the way you make money from stocks or real estate investments. (Stocks can also give you a return on investment by paying out dividends, but we'll get more into that later.)

In both of these situations, you are giving control of your money to someone else for a limited time. In return, at the end of that time, you expect to receive more money than you put in. To earn this extra money in growth or interest, you don't have to do anything extra. You simply let your money go to work for you and you make FREE money.

First, About Interest—How Interesting!

One way you can make your money work for you and earn an ROI is through interest. As we learned in 2.5, paying interest is bad. Interest paid to you, however, is good.

We become so used to borrowing money, that oftentimes the idea of lending our money to make interest ourselves is foreign to us. However, the truth is that the interest coin can be easily flipped. You pay interest to a bank when you borrow money using a credit card. The bank will pay you interest when you let them borrow your money. In fact, whenever you put your money in a basic savings account you are doing just that, although you may not realize it.

Why does a bank want to borrow your money? Don't they have enough? The bank wants to borrow your money because they can use it to make more money. For example, if you put your money in a basic savings account, you may receive ½% or 1% interest, but the bank is lending out that money at 5% or 10% or higher, so it's more than happy to pay you a portion of that. A bank or other financial institution may also want to use your money to fund projects, other companies or endeavors that they believe will provide a return on their investment.

But, if banks are lending out your money in your savings account, how is it still available for you to use? The trick is not to think of your account as a dresser drawer where only your money is tucked away, but to think about the entire bank as a wardrobe in which everyone's money is stored. By pooling everyone's money, the bank maintains a certain amount of overall reserve to make sure that when you wish to withdraw your money, the bank will have the funds.

Interesting Bonds

There are other reasons people may want to borrow your money and pay you interest. For example, a government that needs funds will offer to pay you interest if they can use your money. Or a corporation that needs capital to grow may want to borrow your money in return for regular interest payments. When a government or corporation lends your money in this way, it's called a bond. As sometimes corporations and even governments go broke, lending money to them in a form of a bond is considered more risky than, for example, placing your money in a savings account at your bank. Because it's more risky, it will pay a higher rate of interest.

More Ways to Grow Your Money

Bonds and savings accounts are examples of ways to invest and earn interest off of your money, but earning interest isn't the only way to make your money work for you. When you purchase a stock, your money can grow in two new and interesting ways:

- The stock can grow in value.
- The stock can pay you dividends.

But first, what exactly is a "stock?"

Stocks are generated when a corporation decides to raise money by allowing multiple people ownership in their company. They break up their company ownership into pieces called "shares." The more shares you own, the more pieces of the company you own.

When you a buy a share, you share in the company's successes and losses. If the company is doing well, your share will be worth more. If the company goes bankrupt, your share may be worth nothing. When you buy a share, you are hoping that the company does well and that the value of your share will go up over time, hence providing you a healthy ROI—the growth in your investment.

Of course, some stocks are riskier than others. If you gamble by purchasing shares in a start-up company that no one believes will make it, your purchase price of the share will be low. If the company makes it to the big leagues, the growth in value of the shares could be amazingly high. We've all heard stories of people who are rich today after investing heavily in Microsoft in the '70s.

On the other hand, if you invest in a mature stock such as Microsoft is today, your purchase price may be high and the growth on your investment possibly more limited.

How stocks make you money.

When you purchase a share at say, $5, and in 12 months it is worth $10, then the value of your share has grown. When you sell it, you make a profit. This is the kind of growth that most people think of when they think about stocks.

Many stocks, however, also pay out **dividends**. A dividend is a share of the profits of the company. Companies are not required to pay out dividends, but many of them offer dividends as an incentive for investors to purchase their stock.

Most larger, more stable companies will offer dividends, since the value of the stock may not be expected to grow as quickly as it did during the company's growth stage. For example, if you purchase stock in Wal-Mart, the stock may cost $40 or $60 a share. Their stock value may grow, but even if the value of the stock grows $1 per share in the next year, that is still only a 1.6% return on your money. Therefore, Wal-Mart might sweeten the deal by paying out a portion of their profits in dividends to their investors.

Compound and Reinvest: A Winning Combination

The beautiful thing about investing is that as your money starts to work for you, the money that you earn will begin to work for you as well. So you are soon making a return on your return!

If you leave your money in an interest-bearing account, you'll earn interest on your interest, a process known as "compounding." "Compound interest" means that as you accumulate interest and the total amount of money in your account grows, you'll earn interest not only on the amount you've deposited, but on the interest you've earned as well. That means your interest will be earning interest!

If you've got money in stocks, you can sell shares for a profit, or you can make money in dividends. Then you can use this money to purchase more shares. This process is known as "reinvesting." Compounding or reinvesting creates an exponential snowball effect, and can mean that even at a small return, money left to grow will soon turn into a full-fledged fortune.

Chances are, you'll end up earning through both compounding and reinvesting. Don't worry about the details of how to do all this right now. We'll get into all of that later. Right now, all you need to do is imagine the possibilities!

How do the numbers work in the real world?

But how does this all work in the real world? When you set your money to make money, how much money can it actually make? Millions, of course! We are playing Reality Millionaire, after all.

As shown in the example below, investing just $5,000 (at 10% return) for your child at his or her birth can grow to over $268,000 in 40 years. And that's with just five grand invested one time, imagine what you could do if you invested that five grand every two or three years?

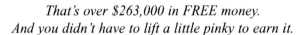

That's over $263,000 in FREE money.
And you didn't have to lift a little pinky to earn it.

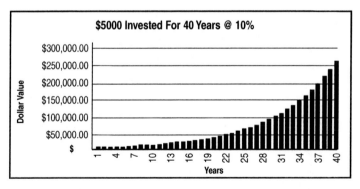

Start Early.
Can You Afford to Wait?

This is an important fact to understand: Investing works better the earlier you start, even if you only invest for a limited time. That means that if you are only going to invest one year in your entire lifetime, it will be better for you to invest in your 20th year than in your 60th. Why? Because when you invest early, the money has more time to generate interest or growth, and as your investments grow, they start earning a return on the return on the return on the return on the return on the return—ok, you get the point.

For example, the chart below demonstrates four hypothetical accounts whose owners contributed $5,000 per year for ten years ONLY. The first one, Joe Genius, started investing at age 25. Over 10 years, he put $5,000 in each year. Then, at 35 he stopped investing and did nothing else but reinvest annually and watch his earnings grow. By age 65, his account balance is at $1,616,955—that's a $1,566,000 return on his original investment.

Our last investor, Joe Late, kept putting off investments. He didn't start investing until he was 55, when he finally felt like he "had a little extra." Joe Late invests for exactly 10 years, just as Joe Genius did, but Joe Late's end account balance at 65 is only a little over $81,000.

That's the power of investing early.

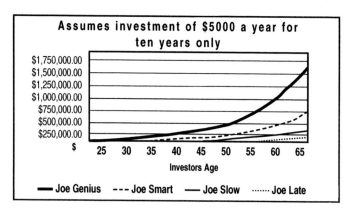

If the advice comes too late, don't panic. It's better to start contributing now than to waste more time thinking about what you didn't do.

Does this really *work?*

But does the Power of Investment really work for the average Joe? What will Joe Average's situation look like after playing Reality Millionaire for a few years? Let's take a look. . . .

JOE AND JANE AVERAGE

Joe and Jane follow their Debt Elimination Plan every month, always putting the same amount into their debts, even as their monthly minimum payments go down. In addition, after saving up for their Emergency Fund, they save the extra money they found from Round Two and put it into accounts that earn 10% interest or growth. After just five years, they are clear of all debt, other than their mortgage, and they have over $28,000 in investments!

<table>
<tr><td>

BEFORE
REALITY
MILLIONAIRE.

Household Income: $44,389
Mortgage: $136,000
Car Loans: $12,000
Other Loans: $3,300
Credit Cards: $8,400

Cash & Investments: Zero.

</td><td>

AFTER JUST 5 YEARS
OF PLAYING
REALITY MILLIONAIRE!

Household Income: $44,389
Mortgage: $114,144
Car Loans: $0
Other Loans: $0
Credit Cards: $0

Cash & Investments: $28,651

</td></tr>
</table>

But wait! That's only the beginning. As soon as Joe and Jane Average are completed with their Debt Elimination Plan, they can put the full amount they were using for their debt into their investments. Look how their account grows!

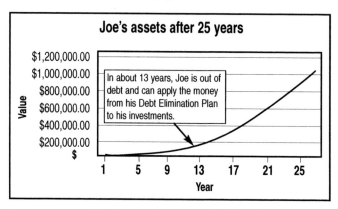

In 26 years, Joe is debt free and has over $1,000,000 in investments.

Let's Do Your Math
Your Fortune-telling Round

Still don't believe me about the Power of Investment? Would you like to see it work with your numbers? Let's do the math and find out where you'll be in the next 20 years.

Surf over to www.realitymillionaire.com and punch in your numbers in our Reality Millionaire Investment Calculator.

To Recap:

• Simply hoarding money (i.e., under your mattress) is not enough to get you to millionaire status.

• To win Reality Millionaire, you must make your money work for you: you must learn how to use the Power of Investment to your advantage.

• There are two basic ways to earn a return on your money: loaning it out in return for interest payments or purchasing something you believe will increase in value or spin off dividends.

• You earn interest when you loan money to a bank or other financial institution.

• When you purchase stocks, your investments don't earn interest, they grow and sometimes pay out dividends.

• As your money begins to generate a return, you can earn more money through compound interest or reinvesting your return.

• Starting early can make a huge difference to your investment future.

• Playing by the simple rules of Reality Millionaire, the average Joe can have a small fortune in investments and be debt free within 20–25 years.

• Do your math. I bet your numbers are just as astounding.

ROUND FIVE

ARE YOU A RISK-TAKER?

Money was never a big motivation for me, except as a way to keep score. The real excitement is playing the game.
—*Donald Trump,* Trump: Art of the Deal

So, down to the nitty gritty. Now that you know that you can make money on your money, how do you do it? Where do you go? What do you invest in? The answer to these questions will depend on your investment style and your current life situation.

As you've read through the last sections, you may have noticed that we've talked about the possibility of some investments generating a greater return than others. There is a basic rule of thumb when determining which investments could generate the greatest profits. You will obtain the possibility of a higher rate of return if you are willing or able to:

- Accept more risk.
- Tie up your money for a longer period of time.

Towards the beginning of your investment life, your options may be limited. After all, not all of us have large sums of money lying around that we can tie up for several years. As you start off, you may also be leery of accepting too much risk. You will probably be looking for some options that will gain you a higher return than a basic savings account, but that will also be fairly low-risk.

But what exactly are your options? Before you begin to peruse them, your first step is to determine what kind of investor you are—then you'll know which options are right for you. You'll find that investing is as personalized as home décor or politics. The same investing style is not suited to everyone. Some people enjoy the fast and furious pace of an aggressive stock portfolio; others prefer the slow but steady advance of safer, low-risk investments.

Your next steps to investment success:

1. Understand which kinds of basic investment options are open to you.

2. Match yourself—your lifestyle, preferences, and current situation—to the right investment style.

What investment options are there?

Where can you put your money? When we think of investments, most of us think about the wild rollercoaster stories of the stock market—the Great Depression, the recent recession, the Roaring '20s, the dot-com boom. But there are several other options besides stocks (some safer than others): treasury bonds and notes, money market accounts, mutual funds, savings bonds, and more.

Sound complicated? The terminology can get confusing, but when you understand the basics it becomes a lot simpler.

Broadly speaking, there are three kinds of assets in which you can invest:

low risk		Asset Type	Examples
Cash *Stable Value Investments.* Cash assets do not necessarily have to be cash, but they are assets that can be converted to cash easily and without large penalties. These are the safest forms of investment. This safety, however, comes with a price: a low rate of return. Sometimes the rate of return can even be lower than the rate of inflation!		Cash stable, converted to cash easily.	CDs Treasury Bills Money Market Accounts
Bonds *Fixed Investments* When you purchase a bond, you are loaning your money to a government or company. The company promises to pay back that bond with interest. Higher interest typically means greater risk. Lower interest—such as you'll receive with government bonds— means a lower return, but a safer one.		Bonds a loan from a government or corporation.	Corporate bonds Municipal bonds Treasury Bonds
Stocks *Equity* When you invest in a stock, you are literally buying part of a company— sort of a mini-partnership. When the company does well, the stock price typically rises in value (growth). If the company does badly, the stock price typically falls. The risk is greater, but there is potential for a higher return.	high risk	Stocks part ownership in a company.	Any of the names you see on the stock ticker on CNN

Mutual Funds Are Any Combination of All Three

A mutual fund is a combination of investment types. It can include stocks, bonds and cash, or it can have just bonds, or just stocks, or just stocks and bonds, or any combination of the three kinds of assets.

> More than 80 million people—that's half of all U.S. households invest in mutual funds.
> —Investopedia.com

Mutual funds come in all sorts of flavors. You can get a mutual fund that only includes technology stocks. Or you can get a mutual fund that has only money market accounts, or only blue chip stocks, or one that has a hodgepodge of investments, which may include stocks, bonds and cash.

The best thing about mutual funds is that they will help you to diversify your assets and keep you from putting too many eggs in one basket. Even if you have an all-stock mutual fund, you are still more diversified than you would be with a single stock; while some stocks may be doing badly in your mutual fund, others may be doing well. This gives you a better chance of attaining a steady return on your investment.

Unless you're a professional day trader, you'll rarely choose to invest in a single stock or bond. For the beginning investor, most of your investments should probably be in mutual funds.

Diversification is the Key to Investment Success

Investing in a single stock or bond is risky. If you try to play the stock market head-to-head with the investment gurus, you'll almost always come out with less money than you put in. A critical key to investing is to diversify properly.

Your first inclination when you hear that mutual funds include a variety of investments may be to pick a fund and go with it. "OK, I know I'm low risk, so I'll get that low-risk fund and that's that." It's diversifying my investments for me, right? Yes and

> There are over 10,000 mutual funds in North America. That means there are more Mutual Funds than stocks!
> *Investopedia.com*

no. If you were only to invest in a single low-risk mutual fund, your overall rate of return could be low—too low. You might prefer low risk, but you still want to maximize your dollars, right?

Investing in a single mutual fund is less risky than investing in a single stock, but it still has its drawbacks. That's because different mutual funds have different levels of risk. High-risk funds tend to include a lot of stocks. High-risk funds may especially contain stocks of small companies that are not yet well established. Low-risk funds diversify more among asset types and include a healthy mix of bonds, cash and less risky stocks, such as those from blue chip companies like Microsoft or Coca-Cola. One of the best ways to diversify is to purchase multiple mutual funds, some low risk, some high risk, and some in the middle. All of your funds and assets together make up what is called your **portfolio**. When you invest in several mutual funds and create a portfolio, you can think of yourself as being doubly diversified. Each mutual fund includes a variety of investments, and your portfolio now contains a variety of mutual funds.

Still hard to visualize?

If this is an Individual Asset…	Then, this is a Mutual Fund…	And This is Your Portfolio…
◊	$◊▲◊ ▲◊ ◊	(diagram of multiple mutual funds with various assets)
Legend: ◊ Stock ▲ Bond $ Cash		

As you can see from the diagram, all of the mutual funds have different mixtures of assets.

- **Bond/Income Funds.** The funds that have high levels of cash and bond assets are known as "Bond/Income Funds." These funds are intended to protect your investment from inflation and provide you with a steady, secure income.

- **Balanced Funds.** The funds known as "Balanced Funds" will be more equally divided between stocks and bonds and are made to balance risk while providing a greater return on investment over the long haul than the Bond/Income Funds.

- **Equity Funds.** The "Equity Funds" are heavy in stocks and focused on long-term growth. They count on the fact that stocks may experience heavy variations in value in the short term, but that the stock market overall has always had many more good years than bad.

Another reason to diversify and purchase a variety of mutual funds is to ensure that your portfolio is well balanced between stock-heavy funds and bond-heavy funds. This is because typically when stocks are doing well, the bonds market will be sagging, and vice/versa. Hence, it's important to be well diversified, so you can ride out the years when the stock market is down and bonds are doing better.

How do you choose a portfolio?

Some people are into skydiving. Others prefer tea and crumpets. How risky are you? Before you can begin forking over some investment dollars in an investment portfolio, you need to determine the style of investment that will be best suited to you. We call this your **risk profile.** Once you know your risk profile, you can match yourself up with an investment portfolio profile that makes sense for you. There are many mutual fund companies that offer ready-made portfolios that match certain risk profiles, from "very conservative" to "very aggressive."

There are two primary factors that go into determining your risk profile:

- Your personal aversion to risk
- The time you have until retirement

 The Risk Rule of Thumb:
The closer you are to retirement, the less risk you should take.

So, even if you are the kind of person who likes to go out on a limb, if you're five years from retirement, it would be an extremely risky proposition to invest your money in a high-risk portfolio. On the other hand, the farther away you are from retirement, the more risk you can afford to take.

Why take risk at all?

Naturally, if everyone could have a great return on investment at a low risk, everyone would do it. But higher risks come with greater potential return on investment. The lower risk portfolios will protect your investments against inflation, but not generate as great a return. What level of risk do you prefer? Take the Risk Profile Quiz below and we'll find out what type of investing style best suits you.

Determine Your Risk Profile: The Risk Profile Quiz

1. Which one best describes you?

    A. I like to play high stakes. The thrill of the game is in how much I can win or lose.

    B. I like to take a gamble now and then, but I get nervous if too much is on the line.

    C. I still play for toothpicks on Poker Night.

2. How many years do you have until retirement?

    A. 15 or less.
    B. 16 to 25.
    C. 26 or more.

3. How set are you on your retirement date?

    A. Very. I will do everything needed NOT to have to work past my planned retirement date.

    B. I really love my work. In fact, I don't really have a set retirement date at all, and I might work some during retirement anyway.

C. I would prefer to retire on my planned retirement date, but if I have to work a few more years, it's not going to break me.

4. How secure do you feel in your present situation?

A. Pretty good. It's hard to save for investments, but I'm not hanging by the skin of my teeth either.

B. Not very. I worry about making ends meet, and squeezing out enough money for this investment stuff is really hard.

C. Very. My Great Aunt Matilda left me a trust fund. I never worry about having enough money.

5. After investing in an initial portfolio, how will you most likely act?

A. I'll be checking it every day. If it loses value, it'll nag at me all night.

B. I'll check it often, but I'll only worry if it seems to steadily lose value over several months.

C. I'm in for the long haul. I'll check it on a regular schedule to rebalance it as needed, but I'm comfortable with riding out the bad with the good.

Grade Yourself

For each answer, give yourself the appropriate number of points:

1. A, 3. B, 2. C, 0.
2. A, 0. B, 2. C, 3.
3. A, 0. B, 3. C, 2.
4. A, 2. B, 0. C, 3.
5. A, 0. B, 2. C, 3.

Now add up your score: _____.

Match yourself with the appropriate risk profile below:

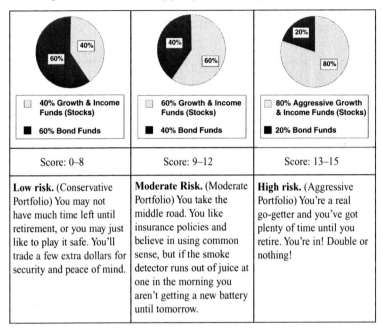

☐ 40% Growth & Income Funds (Stocks)	☐ 60% Growth & Income Funds (Stocks)	☐ 80% Aggressive Growth & Income Funds (Stocks)
■ 60% Bond Funds	■ 40% Bond Funds	■ 20% Bond Funds
Score: 0–8	Score: 9–12	Score: 13–15
Low risk. (Conservative Portfolio) You may not have much time left until retirement, or you may just like to play it safe. You'll trade a few extra dollars for security and peace of mind.	**Moderate Risk.** (Moderate Portfolio) You take the middle road. You like insurance policies and believe in using common sense, but if the smoke detector runs out of juice at one in the morning you aren't getting a new battery until tomorrow.	**High risk.** (Aggressive Portfolio) You're a real go-getter and you've got plenty of time until you retire. You're in! Double or nothing!

Now that you're equipped with your risk profile and you know what kind of portfolio will suit you, you are ready to invest. Finally! In Round Six, you will begin your journey as a Real Investor.

To Recap:

- There are three kinds of basic investment assets: stocks, bonds and cash.

- Mutual funds are a combination of assets and can include stocks, bonds and cash.

- Investing in a mutual fund is usually less risky than investing in a single stock or bond.

- Investing in several differently allocated mutual funds is often less risky than investing in a single mutual fund.

- When you choose several different asset types and mutual funds to invest in, you are building a portfolio and spreading out your risk.

- No matter how much you diversify, you will never eliminate all risk.

- Before you begin to build your portfolio, you need to determine whether you are in a position to build a high-risk portfolio, or whether your lifestyle is better suited to a low-risk portfolio.

- The closer you are to retirement, the less risk you should take.

- You can find out your risk profile by taking the Risk Profile Quiz starting on page 51. Once you know your risk profile, you can begin to build your portfolio.

ROUND SIX

SECURE YOUR RETIREMENT DREAMS.
LET'S INVEST!

If you would be wealthy, think of savings as well
as getting. —Benjamin Franklin

As a wise investor, your next step is to secure your retirement. Just like we took care of your short-term security with the Emergency Fund, we are now going to take care of your long-term security with a Retirement Plan. Both long-term and short-term security are essential to winning Reality Millionaire. After all, how can you build your fortune without a solid foundation? Financial security is the first step to financial freedom.

After you've completed your Emergency Fund, you're going to use the extra money you found from Round Two (at least 10% of your current income) to fund your Retirement Plan. Luckily, 10% is commonly the amount recommended by retirement planners to put away for your retirement goals, depending on age.

You've already completed several steps that will help you put together your Retirement Plan. In Round Five, you matched yourself up with a risk profile and you learned about the benefits of diversifying your investments through a mutual fund portfolio. From Round Four you know the power of earning a return on your return. From Round Two, you've got extra money burning a hole in your pocket. You're ready to go! But where exactly are you going? Should you just call a broker or bank and start buying mutual funds? Well, you can, but there is a better way to invest in your retirement, at least for starters.

You see, if you do it right, you can invest in a Retirement Plan and pay less in taxes. By creating special kinds of accounts, the government has provided tax breaks for people who are investing for their retirement. The two most well known of these are the IRA and the 401(k). These two kinds of accounts will typically provide the best long-term options, and because of the tax breaks the government provides with these accounts, you'll be able to make more on your investments than you would otherwise.

But what are these accounts exactly?

401(k)

A 401(k) is a retirement account that is offered by many employers. There are three big benefits to a 401(k):

1. It is tax-deferred, which means that you won't be taxed on your contributions to your 401(k) or the interest that it earns until you begin to withdraw it from the account.

2. Your employer will often match part of your contribution to your 401(k), sometimes doubling or tripling the total amount you have for retirement several years down the road.

3. Your contributions to your 401(k) come off of the top of your income, so you could end up in a lower tax bracket and owe Uncle Sam less money.

IRA

An IRA is a retirement account that anyone can open, whether or not your employer offers a retirement plan. Here are your big benefits with the IRA:

1. It is tax-deferred or tax-exempt depending on which kind of IRA you choose. (Traditional IRAs are tax deferred. Roth IRAs are tax exempt.) So you can either avoid taxes now and pay them later, or you can pay taxes now and avoid taxes later.

2. You can invest in anything you want as long as you keep the money within the IRA, and you will still receive these tax breaks.

An *asset* is the type of investment such as stocks, bonds, cash or mutual funds; an *account* is where you keep the investment.

You've been dealing with assets and accounts much of your life, though you may not have realized it. When you deposit cash into your checking account, for example: The cash is your asset. The checking account is the account.

In truth, there are many, many different kinds of assets and many, many different kinds of accounts, but you don't have to know about all of them to make good, sound decisions with your hard-earned dollars.

For right now, in Round Six, your easiest (and almost always best) account options for retirement investing will be a 401(k) or an IRA, depending on which is available to you. To further simplify things, we'll assume that your assets at this stage of the game will be mutual funds. We'll talk about the many other things you can do with your money later, but for the moment we are going to start with the . . .

Three Can't-Fail Steps for the Burgeoning Investor

Bet you thought we'd never get here. But here we are, taking your first steps as a Real Investor. Remember after you finished building your Emergency Fund and I said that you'd get to do something FUN with that money later? Well here we are!

We are now going to use the extra money that you found in Round Two to start building your investment portfolio. That extra money is the amount you are going to invest EVERY month, without fail, into your Retirement Plan. Stick to it, and after a while you'll never even notice it's missing from your monthly budget. In fact, whenever possible, work out automatic withdrawals from your paycheck into your investment plan. After all, if you never have the money in hand, you won't spend it.

Now, are you ready to invest? Let's go!

Step 1: Choose an IRA or a 401(k).

Step 2: Create your portfolio.

Step 3: Invest the same amount every month.

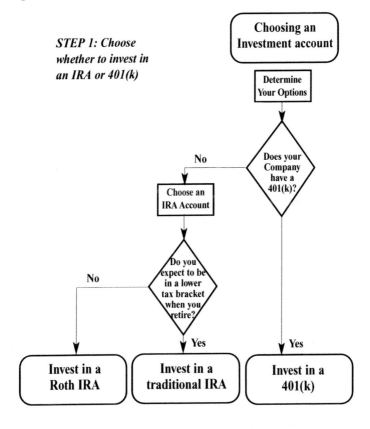

STEP 1: Choose whether to invest in an IRA or 401(k)

Frequently Asked Questions, Step 1:
Should I always go with a 401(k) over an IRA?

Unless you feel your 401(k) plan does not allow you to diversify your assets to your needs, I suggest you always go with a 401(k). Not only does a 401(k) have the added benefit of employer contributions, but if you are eligible for a 401(k), you may not be able to receive your tax break with your IRA account depending on your income.

The flowchart told me to go with either a Traditional or Roth IRA, but I don't understand the difference.

A traditional IRA is tax deferred and you pay taxes when you withdraw the money. A Roth IRA is tax exempt, so you pay taxes before you put the money in. For more detailed information, check out Appendix A.

How to Build Your Portfolio

Step 2:
Create Your Portfolio

Choose your account

In Step 1 above, did you choose to invest in a 401(k)?

No — Go to your bank and open an IRA account

Ask for information on mutual funds for your new account

Yes — Request Information about your plan from your employer

Does your bank or 401(k) plan offer pre-made portfolios?

No — You will need to create your own portfolio

Review the mutual funds available

Choose several mutual funds, picking aggressive, moderate or conservative funds in the correct percentages to match your risk profile*

Yes — Do you feel comfortable with the portfolio offered?

Yes — Invest in the portfolio that matches your risk profile*

* Use the risk profile as determined in round 5.

Frequently Asked Questions, Step 2:
What if I need to open an IRA, but my bank doesn't offer mutual funds at all?

Some banks only provide investment vehicles such as CDs or money market accounts, but they can usually refer you to another financial institution that will be able to open an IRA for your mutual funds.

What if, after reviewing the Mutual Fund information, I still don't know which one to choose?

Don't worry, just ask. Most banks and mutual fund companies will have someone there to help you. They understand that not everyone is knowledgeable about investments. Pick up the phone and give them a call. Let them know how soon you plan to retire and explain what sort of risk profile you've matched yourself up with. They'll be able to recommend the right mutual fund portfolio for you.

What if I maxed out my 401(k) or IRA? They have limits, right?

Congratulations! You're ahead of the game! Yes, they do have limits. If 10% of your income is higher than the limits on your 401(k) or IRA account, you'll need to open a separate investment account, through a brokerage, for example. We'll talk more about additional investment options in Round Seven.

What if my bank doesn't offer premade portfolios, but I don't want to take the time to build my own?

When creating your retirement portfolio, it's often easier to work with your bank. You know them, and you are already a current customer, so they may be more likely to give you the personal service you need. However, if your bank doesn't offer premade portfolios, and you don't want to deal with choosing diversified assets for your portfolio, you aren't out of options. You can choose a premade portfolio that matches your risk profile from most major brokerages or directly from mutual fund companies. Don't worry if you aren't sure how to do that. In Round Seven, I'll walk you through choosing the right companies to help with your investments.

Step 3: Invest the same amount each month. Sit back and watch your earnings grow.

 When you invest the same amount each month, you are not only making things easier to manage, you are taking advantage of **Dollar Cost Averaging**—a technique that takes the guesswork out of trying to "time the market."

You see, mutual funds, like stocks, are sold in **shares**. In the case of stock, one share represents one unit of ownership in a company. So, for example, if a company's stock is split up into 1,000 shares, and you own one of those, then you own 1/1,000th of the company. Shares work similarly in mutual funds. Each share you own represents one unit of ownership in the mutual fund. If the mutual fund has 1,000 shares and you own one share, then you own 1/1,000th of the mutual fund.

If the investments included in the mutual fund are doing well, your shares will be worth more. If they are doing badly, your shares will be worth less.

So, you might think, if mutual funds are bought and sold just like stocks, shouldn't you "buy low and sell high?" Doesn't that mean that you should be investing more in the months when your mutual fund shares cost less? Ah ha! But, unless you are a professional day trader, the chances of your beating the game this way are almost nil. You don't have the time to monitor every nuance of the market. You have a life!

You've got to figure out another way to take advantage of investing that doesn't leave you biting your nails and sitting on the edge of your seat. That way is Dollar Cost Averaging. Forget about trying to beat the market—just invest the same amount every month and you'll come out ahead. Here's how:

Joe Average Uses Dollar Cost Averaging

For example, lets say that Joe Average invests $350 of the extra money that he found from Round Two into his mutual fund portfolio. When his mutual funds are doing well, the price per share is more, so he can afford fewer shares with his $350. When his mutual funds aren't so hot, the price per share is less, so he can afford more shares with his $350.

After several months or years, he will come out ahead of the game. The average cost that he paid for each of his shares will typically be less than the average share cost.

The concept is a little hard to get a hold of, I know. Let's get more specific. The chart below represents Joe Average's investments over four months. In Month One, we see that the share price for his mutual fund portfolio was $10. He had $350 to invest, so he bought 35 shares.

In Month Two, the shares are cheaper, only $6. Now he can buy 58 of them with $350! In Month Three, he was able to purchase even more. In Month Four, the value of the shares started to rise again, and he was able to purchase only 38 with his $350.

Month	Investment	Share Price	Number of Shares Bought	Total Number of Shares Owned
1	$350	$10	35	35
2	$350	$ 6	58	93
3	$350	$ 4	87	180
4	$350	$ 9	38	218

By the end of Month Four, Joe Average had purchased 218 shares in his mutual fund portfolio and he spent a total of $1,400.

Joe Average's Average Cost Per Share: $1,400 / 218 = $6.42. Average Cost of a Share Over the Last Four Months: ($10 + $6 + $4 + $9) / 4 = $7.25.

This example shows that even though the price per share went down, as it does at times, the overall return is still positive. In fact, Joe has spent only $1,400 for 218 shares that at current prices are worth $1,962. So, he's $562 ahead in this example.

In other words, by investing the same amount each month, Joe further minimizes his downside risk and maximizes his potential return.

Frequently Asked Questions for Step 3:
Does Dollar Cost Averaging guarantee a return
on my investment?

No, but over time it will typically help generate a better return than can be achieved through a one-time investment or trying to "time" the market. If the mutual fund portfolio does badly over time, you can still lose money. However, if your portfolio is well diversified and you stick with your plan and continue to make purchases through "slump" periods, chances are, you'll do exceptionally well when the market comes back around— and it always has, given time.

The idea of mutual funds still scares me. How safe
is this, really?

No one can guarantee the safety of your investments. But we can look at history. It is a time-proven fact that since the early days of the stock market, the market has gone up approximately 72% of the time and down 28% of the time, which means if you simply employ a long-term strategy and weather the bad with the good, you'll come out ahead in the long run. The S&P 500 has returned approximately 10% per year over the last 50 years. . . .Once you've chosen the right portfolio for you, you need to be patient. Even the safest portfolio may show loss in some years, but overall, given time, a well-balanced portfolio will grow.

Do I really have to do all of this myself?

No. Many of the mutual fund companies or 401(k) administrators have people that are available to help you. Or you may choose to work with a financial planner. In the chapter "How to Choose a Financial Planner," we'll talk about typical fee structures and the questions you will want to ask them before you retain their services.

Three "Can't-Fail" steps, huh? So what's the catch?

Too easy, right? Actually, yes. There is a catch. 401(k)s and IRAs are retirement plans, which means that you can't withdraw any of your investment money until retirement. If you do, you'll face financial penalties for early withdrawal (10% plus your regular income tax).

Feel a little cheated? What if you want to make the big bucks before you retire? Do you have to wait until you are 50 to go on your dream vacation? That seems unfair! Don't panic. All is not lost. You'll be able to take that vacation earlier than you think. Just keep playing.

To Recap:

- Your Emergency Fund provides for your short-term security. Your Retirement Plan provides for your long-term security.

- Both long-term and short-term security are vital to winning Reality Millionaire.

- One of the easiest ways to start investing in a Retirement Plan is to open up a 401(k) or IRA account.

- These accounts will give you a tax break while you are saving for retirement.

- You may purchase many different kinds of assets to go into these accounts: stocks, bonds, CDs, mutual funds, etc.

- A diversified mutual fund portfolio that matches your risk profile as determined in Round Five will be one of the best options when choosing assets to purchase for your 401(k) or IRA account.

- To start investing in your Retirement Plan, you can follow these three simple steps:

- Step 1: Choose an IRA or a 401(k).

- Step 2: Open the IRA or 401(k) and purchase a mutual fund portfolio that matches your risk profile.

- Step 3: Invest the same amount every month.

- By investing the same amount every month, you take advantage of Dollar Cost Averaging, which takes the guesswork out of playing the market.

- IRAs and 401(k)s are both retirement accounts, which means that you will not be able to withdraw your investment or its earnings without a penalty until you come to retirement age (59 1/2).

ROUND SEVEN

PLAYING IN THE BIG LEAGUES

Money doesn't always bring happiness. People with ten million dollars are no happier than people with nine million dollars.
– Hobart Brown

You've been so good so far, following the rules of Reality Millionaire, modifying your finances to make room for investments, paying off your debt, and putting away diligently for your retirement. I bet you feel pretty good about yourself, and you should.

Time for a pat on the back . . . let's recap what we've done so far:

1) You've found extra money in your current finances for investments.

2) You've built an Emergency Fund, bringing you a much-needed level of security.

3) You are well on your way down the path of your Debt Elimination Plan.

4) You are following The Golden Rule of Credit Card Use.

5) You're investing in your retirement in an IRA or 401(k) account with investments that match your risk profile.

Wait! Where are we getting all of this money again? How are we getting out of debt and investing and funding an emergency fund? I know, we've been on quite a financial adventure already. But it's really quite simple.

Use the extra money from Round Two to:

1. Build the Emergency Fund
2. Then fund your Retirement Plan

Get out of debt by:
  • Committing to your current minimum monthly debt payment and paying this as a fixed payment every month (even as your minimum payments decrease).

Congratulations! You are almost done. But . . . what about that family vacation to Maui? If you spend your extra money every month on a retirement plan, when do you get to enjoy all of this money you're earning? Never fear. We still have a few more rounds left.

Oh good! So, you might be thinking, does that mean I really don't have to invest all of the extra money in an IRA or 401(k)? Caught you. Thinking about breaking the rules already? Sorry, to win Reality Millionaire, you really do have to spend the extra money (at least 10% of your current income) in your retirement plan. But there is still a way for you to save up for your big Life Goals that you sketched out way back in Round One.

You see, you have access to more money than you think you do, and there are three ways to get it:

Opt to save more than 10% of your income every month.

Try looking for other ways to cut, and I bet you can easily save 15% in frivolous expenses. That's 10% you can use for your retirement fund and 5% you can use investing towards Life Goals. After all, would you rather have chocolate ice cream for dessert every evening or would you rather take that cruise you've always wanted? Face it: chocolate ice cream isn't that good for you anyway.

Earn more through an extra odd job here and there.

You'd be surprised how many little things you can do to pick up some extra cash. Rather than letting your extra earnings burn a hole in your pocket, put them in investments to meet your Life Goals. You can get some more ideas about this in the Extra Income section.

Sit back and wait for all the extra money to come in after you finish your Debt Elimination Plan.

Remember, Joe Average pays out over $1,400 in debt every month. That's a hefty sum that will all be yours just as soon as you stop owing other people money.

To start investing towards your Life Goals, choose one of the above ways to find some extra dough, and we'll use it to make LOTS of extra dough. But how? Just keep doing what you're already doing. Invest in mutual funds, always keeping your investments in line with your risk profile. There is only one major difference now that you're investing in something outside of retirement: You now need a new kind of account.

Before, for retirement investing, your account was an IRA or a 401(k). But you can't save towards your Life Goals in these accounts - because these accounts are for retirement. Remember, you can't touch them without paying a penalty until you are 59½ or older. You need to get a new kind of account in which to put your other mutual fund investments.

But where do you get the account you need for your new Life Goal investments in mutual funds? You have four basic options at this point. These differ in the costs associated with the option and the amount of help you receive in your investment decisions.

1. Hire a Financial Planner.

If you feel uncomfortable making decisions about your money or just don't feel you have the time or background to learn about individual mutual fund companies or brokerages without a guiding hand, a financial planner may be the best option for you. A financial planner will go above and beyond simply advising you on your mutual fund portfolio. They will help you find the right brokerage or mutual fund company to hold your accounts, and they will provide many additional services including helping you plan your estate, ensuring that you are properly insured and assisting you in preparing a will.

2. Purchase Direct.

Most mutual fund companies will allow you to purchase directly, and many offer pre-made portfolios that will fit your risk profile.

The advantage to this is that you pay only the fee that the mutual fund charges for management of the fund. If you want to sell, you sell the shares back to the company at their current market value. There are no extra costs involved. As long as you can find a mutual fund company that offers a portfolio that matches your risk profile, and you feel comfortable with their options, purchasing direct can be a good way to go.

The downside of purchasing directly is the possibility of having to set up several different accounts with different mutual fund companies in the event that one company does not match your profile to your liking.

3. Discount Brokerage Accounts.

Brokerage companies are middlemen; they negotiate your sale or purchase with Wall Street. Unless you purchase directly, they're hard to get around completely. Years back, if you wanted to invest in mutual funds, you had to go to an expensive full service brokerage. But, as investing has become less and less the privilege of the rich and more and more a necessary part of Joe Average's life, more options have opened up.

Discount brokerages have become the brokerage options for the average Joe. The downside? They'll offer limited advice as to which mutual fund you should pick. Their advantages are their relatively low fees ($5 to $30 per transaction, some available without transaction fees), the ability to purchase a wide selection of funds in one place, and their easy online access that allows you to buy and sell individual mutual funds, stocks and bonds without running down to the trading pit.

4. Full Service Brokerage Accounts.

Full service brokerages will typically cost more per trade, but will give you more advice, even helping you with retirement planning and tax tips. You'll have a personal broker with whom you talk and discuss your proposed purchases and sales. They'll be able to give you advice on specific funds based on your profile, as well as provide you full access to extensive investment-related research.

Brokerages and financial planners vary widely in their fee structures, their minimum deposits and their methods of operation. Brokerages have a wide range of minimum deposits, monthly fees, transaction fees and commissions. Financial planners may charge you by the hour, may have a flat fee per service, may work on commission or may ask for a percentage of your investment.

So, what next?

This Round of Reality Millionaire is a bit of a choose-your-own-adventure. Remember those? The books where you get different endings depending on which choices you made? You are now doing the same thing with your real-life financial choices. Here's your chance to recapture your childhood and. . . .

Choose Your Own Financial Adventure!

When the mailman comes, you're sitting on the couch with a bag of Ruffles, munching away and reading a rather off-the-wall book on finances that is trying to convince you that money managing is fun. You see the post guy in his blue suit through the slits in the Venetian blinds, and although the book is hard to put down —it's got your head filled with dreams of sunny beaches and large bank accounts—you decide to get up and check the mail for checks. After all, if there's one from Ed McMahon, you wouldn't have to worry about this mutual funds chapter you're reading. Or, then again, maybe you'd have more reason than ever to finish up the book, so you'd know what to do with your money.

Coming back in from the box, you flip three pieces of junk mail in the trash, shuffle a bill under a pile on your foyer desk and take three small pamphlets to the couch with you. Darn, no checks. But these three pamphlets caught your eye since you were just trying to figure out where you should go to purchase mutual funds.

"How to Choose a Financial Planner," you read the first tagline aloud. The next envelope reads: A Do-It-Yourself Pocket Guide to Buying Mutual Funds Directly. The last piece is headlined What to Look for in the Perfect Brokerage.

It's your adventure. You can read through all of them, or you can choose to read only the one you are interested in. Which piece of mail do you read?

   A. The one about How to Choose a Financial Planner. You decide you don't much like dealing with the numbers your-self. You'd rather hire a professional to do it. Read page 73.

B. The Do-it-Yourself Pocket Guide to Buying Mutual Funds Directly. You don't need anyone between yourself and your money. You'll buy your mutual funds directly. Turn to page 77.

C. What to Look for in the Perfect Brokerage. You think you like the idea of having a broker. You could start with a good online discount brokerage and maybe move on to a full service brokerage later as you have more to invest. Turn to page 88.

Or just read on, and then make your decision once you have determined which is the best for you.

Choosing a Financial Planner: Eeeny Meeny Miny Money

Each year, come April, we rely on ourselves or our tax advisors to get our year's taxes squared away. But what about the rest of the year, and all those years to come? A financial planner is someone who can assist you with your long- and short-term financial goals, providing valuable expert advice. "But I know what I am doing," you may be thinking, "I know how to balance my checkbook and pay my bills. Why do I need help from a stranger?" The aid of a financial planner can offer an experienced perspective on your financial situation and guide you step-by-step towards achieving the financial goals that right now may seem like pipe dreams.

A financial planner is a qualified professional whose job it is to advise you on making big decisions with your money. He or she should be knowledgeable about all financial options, including things a broker may not have much experience with, such as estate planning and will preparation, cash flow management and insurance policies. The benefit of having a financial planner is to create a long-term working relationship with an individual who has your best interests at heart when it comes to your money, and will advise you wisely according to your personal objectives.

A financial planner is also an investment advisor. Instead of trying to sort through the murky, complex world of stocks, funds and bonds yourself, a financial planner acts as your personal advisor, one-on-one, so you can rely on expert guidance instead of constantly worrying about whether your own decisions are informed enough to meet your investment goals.

But how do you choose the person you will trust to help you with something as important as your hard-earned money? First of all, you need to be aware that practically anyone can call himself or herself a "financial planner." The professional-sounding title doesn't guarantee professional quality service. You need to do your homework and make sure that any financial planner you consult is a Certified Financial Planner™ (CFP®), a Personal Financial Specialist (PFS), or a Chartered Financial Consultant® (ChFC®).

What's it gonna cost me?

Since we are talking about money, we ought to talk about the cost of using the services of a financial planner. What's the damage? Well, not all financial planners are paid in the same way. Some are fee-based, some are commission-based, and some are both. If a financial planner works for a flat or hourly fee, he or she is considered a fee-based planner; you are paying directly for his or her services.

Commission-based planners are usually more affordable, but they also have something to gain from your use of their advice. That considered, commission-based planners could offer advice that may be biased, because they want something out of it, too. They typically charge you a percentage of the total money they are managing for you.

One type is not necessarily better than the other, but make sure that you ask for a detailed schedule of any and all fees that will be charged for the financial planning services. If you don't understand the fee structure, don't be afraid to ask the planner to explain it.

How do I find the right planner for me?

There are five questions you should always ask any financial planner before deciding to team up with him or her. This is going to be a long-term relationship, so you want it to be reliable, and enjoyable:

1. What is your education in financial planning?
  How much experience do you have?

Again, you want to be sure that your financial planner is certified and well experienced in the field. He or she may practice as an accountant, or has been to business school, or perhaps has been advising for decades. These are the sort of credentials that are crucial to understanding the quality of the services your financial planner is capable of providing.

2. What are your areas of expertise?

Financial planners wear many hats—they may specialize in retirement planning, estate planning, insurance planning, investment planning, or tax planning. Make sure you choose a financial planner who will best meet your needs.

3. How will I pay for your services?

Remember, a financial planner may be paid a flat or hourly fee, by commission, or by some combination of the two. Know your payment options before committing to financial services. After all, the entire reason you are hiring them is because you care about your money.

4. What is your approach to financial planning?
  Will you be looking at the whole picture, or focusing
  on particular assets? Is your investment philosophy
  aggressive or conservative?

Okay, there are more than five questions. Understanding your financial planner's approach to investments is essential to your choice to allow him or her to manage your finances. After all, it's your money—you should make sure that your financial planner's goals match yours when it comes to how aggressively you want to handle your investments.

5. May I have our agreement in writing?

Be sure to obtain copies of all documents signed by you and your financial planner regarding payment and services. No experienced, ethical financial planner will be offended by this question; it is absolutely your right to keep written documents for your personal records.

Don't forget to do your detective work. For starters, look around on the Internet for information about your potential financial planner. To dig a little deeper, do a background check to make sure that your potential financial planner has never been censured by a licensing board or prosecuted for illegal activities. One easy way to do this is to go to www.nasd.com and click on the "Check Out Brokers & Advisers" link in the Investor Information section. You can never be too careful (or too nosy) when it comes to your assets.

Who puts the "work" in "teamwork?"

Go ahead and ask your financial planner whether this is his or her primary job, and whether others will be assisting in the management of your funds. You would certainly want to know about the credentials of anyone and everyone who is involved in managing your money. It may not just be the person you shake hands with.

As Bette Davis once said: "To fulfill a dream, to be allowed to sweat over lonely labor, to be given a chance to create, is the meat and potatoes of life. The money is the gravy."

Let your financial planner help you make that gravy extra tasty. This is one case where there can be too many cooks. By doing a little research and maintaining high standards, it will be easy to find a financial planner who will help you handle your money with care and give your finances a little flavor.

A Do-It-Yourself Pocket Guide to Buying Mutual Funds Directly

If you've got a do-it-yourself attitude, and you are planning on investing directly with a Mutual Fund Company, the first step is to glance back at Round Five and remember your Risk Profile Quiz. In Round Five, depending on your aversion to risk and the time you have until retirement, you matched yourself with a risk profile.

Aggressive Portfolio

Aggressive Risk Profile for young professionals with strong stomachs.

☐ 80% Aggressive Growth & Growth Funds (Stocks)
■ 20% Bond Funds

Moderate Portfolio

Balanced Risk Profile for those who want security and steady long term growth

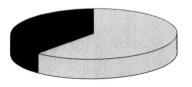

☐ 60% Growth & Income Funds (Stocks)
■ 40% Bond Funds

Conservative Portfolio

Conservative Risk Profile for individuals within 5 to 10 years of retirement.

☐ 40% Growth & Income Funds (Stocks)
■ 60% Bond Funds

If you are close to retirement, you probably chose a conservative risk profile that translates to a conservative mutual fund portfolio—heavy in more secure investments such as cash and bonds. If you are in your 20s or 30s and are willing to take a few chances, you may have chosen an aggressive risk profile and a portfolio weighted towards stocks. The chart on page 77 will give you a quick recap of portfolios that match up with your risk profile.

Once you know how your portfolio will be divided among the different types of assets—cash, bonds and stocks—the next step is to find the right mutual funds to include. For example, imagine if you've chosen an aggressive risk profile. According to the chart, you'll need to purchase funds heavy in stocks to fill up 80% of your portfolio. The rest of your funds, 20%, should be invested in bonds.

There are a two ways to do this:

A. Purchase a premade portfolio that matches your risk profile (for the true couch-potato investor).

B. Create your own portfolio that matches your risk profile (for those who want a little more control).

Purchasing a Premade Portfolio

As more and more Americans are taking charge of their own investments, premade portfolios are gaining in popularity. Whereas it used to take an Einstein (or a wealthy investment specialist) to navigate the complicated world of investment jargon and options, nowadays, anyone can invest by choosing a premade portfolio that matches his or her needs.

You can find premade portfolios at most of the major investment banking firms. These portfolios feature a predetermined mix of bonds, stocks and cash to meet the risk profile you choose. Depending on the firm, the portfolios may be called one-choice portfolios, life-cycle funds, premixed portfolios, one funds, or allocation funds. But no matter the name, the premise is the same: to enable investors to buy and forget.

Each premade portfolio works a little differently, so you'll want to do your homework, but many firms offer portfolios based on your target retirement age. These portfolios automatically rebalance as you near the big date, increasing bonds and decreasing stocks for a more conservative approach as you get older.

Creating Your Own Portfolio

If you are a true investing desperado and don't trust others to properly allocate your investments for you, you'll want to diversify your funds yourself. But where do you get these mutual funds? When buying direct, you know you need to buy directly from a mutual fund company . . . but how exactly do you do that? And how do you choose from the literally thousands of funds available?

Introducing Investing For EVERYONE
The Index Fund

If you don't purchase a premade portfolio, the next most popular solution for the beginning investor is to invest in what are called index funds. An index fund attempts to follow a benchmark for the market—that is, it doesn't try to do any better than the average fund. It simply tries to follow exactly what the market is doing, with all its ups and downs. And since the market is historically up almost 75% of the time, index funds are a pretty good bet.

People who buy index funds are usually passive investors who prefer not to be actively managing their portfolios or to be constantly looking to snatch up the newest and hottest buys on the mutual fund market. Like the Average Joe, they'd rather spend their time in front of the TV, or at Little League, or at the beach, or anywhere but digging through long lists of mutual fund yields, averages and ratings.

Another plus to investing in an index fund is that fees are typically much lower than other mutual funds, since the people in charge of managing the fund follow simple guidelines about which stocks to purchase. The work involved in managing the fund is significantly less than an actively managed fund where fund managers are working hard to buy and sell stocks and bonds at just the right times.

What's all this about fund managing? Why do you have to pay any fees at all? Remember, a mutual fund is a collection of stocks, bonds or cash assets. But someone has to pick which assets go into the fund. That someone is the fund manager. Even when buying direct and not going through a brokerage, you'll still need to pay a fund management fee.

But which Index Fund?

You mean there is more than one? Of course, the world of finances isn't going to let us off that easily. Yes, there are several index funds. Back in 1896, Charles Dow created one of the most famous index funds, the Dow Jones Industrial Average (DJIA), which included 12 of the most financially influential U.S. companies. Since then, a variety of indexes have sprung up as ways to measure the overall state of the financial market. Most of us have seen some of these on the little scrolling stock tickers on the bottom of CNN: DJIA, NASDAQ, Russell 2000, Wilshire 5000, and S&P 500 to name a few.

There are indexes that track the changes in foreign stocks, in small or large company stocks, and in stocks in certain industries. There are also separate indexes for the stock market and the bond market.

Luckily, we don't have to go far when choosing which kind of index fund we want to buy. The easy answer is: Go with the masses.

For stocks. One of the most commonly used benchmarks of the stock market is called the S&P 500, which stands for Standard and

Poor's 500 Index. This is an index consisting of 500 stocks chosen specifically to represent the state of the domestic stock market.

Although the last years have been volatile for stocks, it's important to remember that investment in stock-heavy mutual funds is a long-term investment strategy. In the last 50 years, there have only been three five-year periods in which the S&P 500 has produced a negative return. And the good times have far made up for the losses incurred by the bad.

The S&P Index Since 1960.

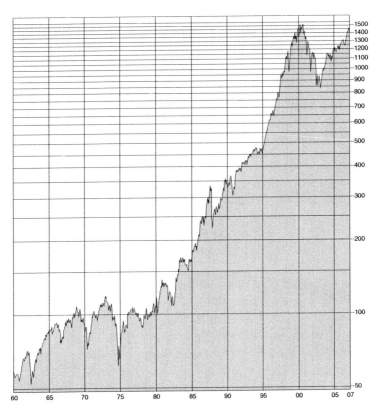

For bonds. One of the most commonly used benchmarks used to track the bond market is the Lehman Brothers Aggregate Bond

Index. This index tracks 6,000 government, corporate, mortgage and asset-backed securities, chosen to mirror the activity of the overall bond market.

Besides being protected against weak years in the stock market, one of the reasons for diversifying into bonds is that when stocks are down, bonds tend to be doing strongly.

Historically, when stocks are down, bonds perform strongly.

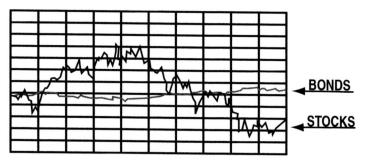

In the early 2000s, the stock market showed a decline.
Returns on bonds, however, went up.

The 1-2-3s of the Index Fund Investing Plan

1. Purchase shares in an S&P Index Fund until you have matched your asset allocation for stocks in your risk profile.

2. Purchase shares in a Bond Index Fund until you have matched your asset allocation for bonds in your risk profile.

3. Purchase shares in a money market or government money fund until you have matched your allocation for cash equivalents in your risk profile.

Voila! You now have a nice, balanced mutual fund portfolio that matches your risk profile. Of course, there are many other options, opinions and strategies when it comes to investing; I can't promise that this strategy will work any better than others. However, it's a darn good way to simplify things and to play the game by the statistics and not by blind luck.

A Joe Average Example

Joe Average has chosen a moderate risk profile. Looking back at his risk profile chart, that means that Joe should have 60% of his portfolio in stocks, and 40% in bonds.
He is going to start by investing $500.00.

Joe is going to invest in the following Mutual Funds to complete his portfolio:

Fund Name	Share Price (Example Only)	Planned Percentage of Portfolio
S&P Index Fund	$10.00	60%
Bond Index Fund	$10.00	40%

Joe wants to invest 60% of his money into stocks that follow the S&P Index Fund. Sixty percent of his $500 investing money is $300, so he does the math and realizes that he can purchase 30 shares at $10.00 with his $300. He purchases 30 shares and moves on to his next purchase.

Joe wants to invest the remaining 40% of his total investment in bonds. At $10.00 per share with $200.00, he can purchase 20 shares in the Total Bond Fund Index.

His portfolio now looks like this:

Moderate Portfolio

- 60% Growth & Income Funds (Stocks)
- 40% Bond Funds

It's so EASY . . . but, where do I get these funds again?

We have the fundamentals down, and you're ready to go purchase some index funds, but where do you do that? If you are going to buy directly, you'll want to start by going to an unbiased source (try Morningstar.com) to compare funds. Then, call the company that manages the fund directly and start buying. Or, you may want to purchase from an online brokerage, covered in the section "What to Look for in the Perfect Brokerage" on page 88.

When you compare funds, you'll notice that multiple companies offer S&P Index Funds. The choice of which company to choose can be daunting, but in most cases these funds will be fundamentally similar. After all, they are all S&P Index Funds that follow strict guidelines to match the performance of the S&P Index.

Your choice between, say, the Vanguard S&P 500 Index Fund and Schwab's S&P 500 Index Fund, is a bit like choosing between Energizer AAA's and Duracell AAA's. They do basically the same thing; the largest differentiator will be your out-of-pocket costs.

> **Tip:** When purchasing any investment, always max out your IRA or 401(k) first. Remember those? The retirement accounts from Round Six? With a 401(k) or IRA you can invest in any asset you want, as long as you keep the money in the account. This includes index funds. And these accounts offer you tremendous tax savings. So, max these out first before you open any other investment accounts.

Reading a Mutual Fund Chart

When you start looking at mutual funds, DON'T PANIC. The overload of information can be daunting, but like anything else in life: Once you understand it, it's easy.

Let's take a quick look at an index fund chart, so that I can show you the basis of how to read these. To check some out yourself, go to Morningstar.com; go to the Tools section and use their Basic Screener. Each fund will have an overview page that looks a bit like the chart below. I've circled the important areas to help explain them.

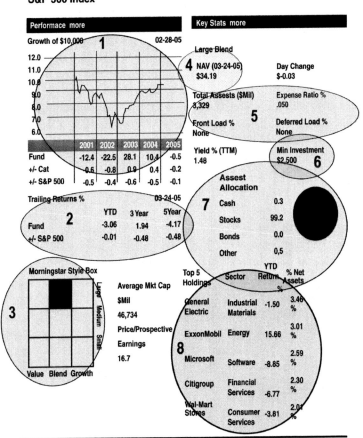

S&P 500 Index

1. Past Performance.

This graph shows the growth (or loss) of the fund over the past several years. In this case, it represents your return on $10,000 invested in the fund from 2001 to 2005. Since this is an S&P Index Fund, it reflects what happened to the stock market in the early 2000s (notice the somewhat scary dip). It may seem counterintuitive to say that the dip is good, but it shows that this fund is doing exactly what it is supposed to be doing: following the stock market through its ups and downs. Remember, an index fund is not trying to second-guess the flow of the market for larger gains (and potentially larger losses); it's trying to mirror the market.

Below the graph, the data indicates how this S&P Index Fund has compared to other S&P Index Funds (shown in the +/- Cat row) and how well it has mirrored the S&P 500 itself (shown in the +/- S&P 500 row). Since the purpose of this fund is to mirror the S&P, the numbers in the Fund row should be close to the numbers in the Category and S&P 500 rows.

2. History of Return.

The data in this area represents how the fund performed over the last three and five years. YTD stands for Year To Date and the negative number indicates that the fund has lost 3.06 percent so far this year. One thing to watch out for: The positive number in year three doesn't necessarily mean that they had a positive return in year three. It means that when you average the last three years together the average return has been positive. This could actually mean that two out of the last three years had a negative return, but that the fund made up for it in one really good year.

3. Morningstar® Style Box.

You won't see this style box on every fund, but you will see it often. This style box represents what category a fund falls into. In the case of S&P Index Funds, all of them will fall into the Large/Blend box, so you won't need to look at this box too closely if you stick only to S&P Index Funds. Large/Blend means that the fund invests in large companies and that the company's stocks are neither primarily growth stock (stock from companies that are out of favor now, but have high potential for growth) or value stock (stock from companies are believed to be undervalued), but that the fund invests in a mix of both value and growth stock.

4. NAV.

NAV stands for Net Asset Value and represents the current price per share.

5. Fund Fees.

All funds have some sort of fees. When you buy a mutual fund, you are pooling your money with a number of other people, which enables you (as part of a group) to pay a professional manager to select the stocks that match the Fund's profile and objectives. The money you pay the manager, as well as other operating costs of the fund—office space, phone lines, etc., is represented by the expense ratio. Anything under .5% is considered low. Front Load and Deferred Load both refer to sales fees that are charged by a broker. There are many "no-load" funds available as well as "loaded" funds. Look at the performance of each fund to determine whether or not it's worth paying for a loaded fund.

6. Minimum Investment.

This is the minimum amount that you can invest in the fund. You'll want to check this number first before you get too far. It's frustrating to find a fund you like, only to find you can't afford it. Many funds have a much smaller minimum investment for investors willing to set up an automatic draft each month.

7. Asset Allocation.

The asset allocation shows that almost this entire fund is invested in stocks (which makes sense since it is a S&P Index Fund created to mirror the stock market). A bond index fund will be composed almost entirely of bonds. Of course there are plenty other non-index funds that are composed of mixtures of stocks, bonds and cash assets.

www.realitymillionaire.com 87

8. Top Holdings.

The top holdings are the top stocks in which the fund has invested.

Once you've compared a few index funds and found some that you like, you'll want to request a prospectus from the ones you are interested in. A prospectus will give you the not-for-the-faint-hearted ins and outs of the fund to help you to make your final decision.

The rest is easy. Simply call the companies in charge of your favorite fund and start buying. Many mutual fund companies will also allow you to purchase online.

Final Tip: Once you've decided how you wish to purchase your funds, I highly recommend setting up an automatic bank draft into your funds each month. It will be MUCH easier than having to write the check every month, and after a month or two you won't even miss the money. Really.

What to Look for in the Perfect Brokerage.

If you've decided to go the brokerage route (instead of going to a financial planner or buying direct), your next step is choosing the right one. The options can seem intimidating. It's a bit like choosing a mechanic or a lawyer. There are good ones out there, but how do you choose the right one? How do you know when their fees are fair for their services? And, most importantly, how do you know if you can trust them with your money?

I once heard a story about a mechanic that sold a woman "headlight fluid," simply because she didn't know any better. If she had taken the time to become a knowledgeable customer, at least on the basics, she could have saved herself $50 and a lot of ridicule at family barbeques. When you start out searching for the right brokerage, you'll probably feel as lost as she was. How do you know when they are trying to sell you a bottle of snake oil? In this section, I'll give you the tools to arm yourself with some basic knowledge, learn the jargon, and know the right questions to ask.

What is a Broker?

Just as Wal-Mart or Neiman Marcus is the middleman between the manufacturer and your next pair of jeans, a broker is the middleman between your investments and the companies that offer them. Just as the salesman at the department store may help you pick out the right size and style in pants, so might a broker help you out with picking the right investments for your portfolio. And just as the saleslady gets a cut when you take home your new pair of Levis, so does the broker get a commission when you buy or sell your investments. In short, a broker is a salesman.

As we discussed earlier, there are full service brokerages (the Neiman Marcuses of the brokerage world) and discount brokerages (the Wal-Marts). If you think you do well enough picking out your own pair of Wranglers, then you'll probably want to hit the clearance racks at Wal-Mart and save some money. If you don't mind the mark-ups at Neimans, and feel you need the extra advice (and pampering), then the fancier department stores will be your thing.

For the most part, if you decide to go with a brokerage, rather than buying direct or choosing a financial planner, you'll probably want to start with a discount brokerage. After all, we aren't millionaires yet—we still have quite a bit of work to do! On the other hand, it's important for you to do what you feel most comfortable with concerning your money. If you feel that a personal broker is more your style, you'll use much of the same criteria in choosing one as you would an online broker.

Online Brokerages: Just a Click Away.
How to Choose an Online Discount Broker

Luckily, if you've decided to go with a discount broker, discount brokerages are easy to find. Online discount brokerages are HOT! Many of us have seen the commercials for Ameritrade, eTrade, Fidelity or Datek. They're in fast-n-furious competition, all promising the best rates, the best Web sites and the best customer service. But how to choose?

The first step to choosing one is to simply start surfing. Go to their Web sites. Which one feels comfortable to you? Which one is the easiest to use? Below is a list of online brokerages to get you started. But don't stop with this list. There are literally thousands to choose from.

Sample Brokerages in Alphabetical Order*		
America First Trader American Century Amex (American Express) Ameritrade Bank One Brown & Co. Charles Schwab CitiTrade Datek Discover Brokerage Direct DLJ Direct	Dreyfus ETrade Fidelity Investments FirstTrade FinancialCafe Harris Direct Merrill Lynch Direct MSDW Muriel Siebert & Co. NDB Quick & Reilly	Scottrade Suretrade T. Rowe Price TD Waterhouse Trading Direct USAA Vanguard Web Street WellsTrade (Wells Fargo) WingspanBank

* I don't endorse any particular brokerage. This list was selected because each of these brokerages was ranked somewhere in a top 10 or 20 brokerage list by either Kiplinger, Forrester, Watchfire GomezPro, USA Today, AAII or TheStreet.com in surveys done over the last seven years.

Narrow Your List

Once you've visited a few broker Web sites, you may have culled a few from your list, but you probably have quite a bit more cutting to do before you reach a final decision. Your next step in narrowing your options is to decide what kind of trader you want to be. Will you be an active trader or a buy-and-hold strategist?

Active Trader (not recommended). If you plan to trade daily or at least weekly, if you plan to try and "play" the market, if you really think you're going to get into this whole day trader thing, then you want to be an active trader. You'll probably care about features like real-time quotes, fast order confirmations, 99.9% uptime, 24-hour trading and massive research archives. You'll need these things because your trades will have to be well-researched and timed to perfection.

Buy-and-Hold Strategist. If you're like the rest of us, and don't really want to mess with finances every day, if you'd be happier in front of the TV or at the gym or at the coffee shop or at Dairy Queen with a banana split, then you want to be a buy-and-hold strategist. You'll be looking for things like customer service, ease of use, comfort, clarity and security.

Get Your Priorities Straight

The easiest way to get started is to line up your priorities.

Use the list below to rank the features of your "dream brokerage."

_____ **Low Commissions and Fees.** Every brokerage will charge fees for trading. After all, that's how they make their money. What you have to decide is how much you are willing to pay for the value of the service they provide. Some brokerages will offer certain funds without a sales charge, such as select no-load, index funds. Other brokerages charge for every trade, no matter what. Some brokerages advertise their clear fee structures and "no hidden charges." Other brokerages will charge you for inactivity, low balances, small transactions, and special order requests. Whichever brokerage you choose, make sure you understand what they will be charging you for, and that you accept those charges as reasonable.

_____ **Ease of Use & Comfort.** Walk through an order or use features on the brokerage site as far as the site will let you without setting up an account. Do you feel like you know what is going on? Do they offer helpful tutorials? Would you feel comfortable making a trade on the Web site?

_____ **Investment Offerings.** Do you need a wide range of investment options? Some brokerages only offer stocks, so if you have a particular investment type or fund in mind, make sure that the brokerage you plan to use offers it. You may also want to check for any premade portfolios that match your risk profile.

_____ **Clarity.** One good way to compare brokerages is to go to Morningstar.com, find a fund that you may be interested in, and then go to the individual brokerage sites and search for the fund's symbol (listed after their name on their profile). Compare how different brokerages display the same fund. Which one is easier to understand? Which one gives you the best information?

_____ **Reliability.** No one likes to think about it, but in an age of technology, things break—especially computers. How reliable is your brokerage's Web site? How often does it go down for routine maintenance (or not so routine maintenance)? How often does it have problems completing trades? Does the online trading system work consistently to make the transactions that you have ordered? Don't be afraid to ask.

_____ **Customer Service.** Hopefully, you won't need them much. The Internet is a wonderful tool, but what happens if there is a problem? Don't you want to know that there will be a voice on the other end of the line? Make sure that there is a phone number on the Web site and call it. If you don't feel comfortable with the service you're getting as a prospective customer, the voice on the other end of the line is not likely to get any friendlier if you have a problem.

_____ **Ease of Cancellation.** This is one that a lot of people forget to ask. Who wants to think about leaving when you just got there? But it's important to know how easy or difficult it will be to close or transfer your account. Customers of some online brokerages have had nightmare stories about being unable to transfer hundreds of thousands of dollars from one account to another. Call customer service and ask what their procedure is for transferring money to other brokerages and how long you could expect to wait before such a transfer will be complete.

_____ **Real-Time Capabilities.** Do they offer real-time portfolio updates, e-mail updates confirming your transactions, and real-time stock quotes? If you're going to be doing some serious and frequent trading, these things could be high on your list of "musts."

_____ **Room to Grow.** Many brokerage firms are part of larger financial firms that offer multiple financial services such as loans, bank accounts, credit cards and financial advice. Are you the kind of person that likes to one-stop shop? If so, it may be important for you to pick a brokerage where you have room to grow.

_____ **News and Research.** Almost every online brokerage will have a plethora of free information, news, research and tutorials on their Website. But once you have an account, many brokerages also offer custom reporting and data. If you're serious about your trading, hard-core statistics might be important to you.

_____ **Security**. By law, every U.S. brokerage must have SIPC coverage, which is basically insurance for up to $500,000 of your investments. Of course, that's only to protect against such things as broker insolvency, not market fluctuations or bad investment decisions. Some brokerages have purchased additional protection for their investors, and if you plan to invest a large sum in one firm, this may be important to you. You may also want to check out the security measures they have taken to protect your personal information and, of course, your accounts.

_____ **Extra Options.** You may be looking for a specific extra option, such as IRA accounts (offered by most brokerages), dividend reinvestment (an option to automatically reinvest your dividends rather than getting a check), or sweep funds (a fund in which any uninvested money left over from a profitable sale, dividends, etc., will be swept into a money market account where it will earn interest).

Get Outside Help

Once you've lined up your priorities, you can probably go through your list of potential brokerages and scratch some out. Hopefully, you're down to just a handful. You'll need a few extra pieces of info before you take that final step.

There are a few places you can go for unbiased information. Here are a few ideas:

- *Ask your friends & family.* Ask people you know what brokerage they use. Are they happy with it? Have they ever had any problems? Were the issues satisfactorily resolved?

- *"Google" It.* There are a ton of forums out there discussing pros and cons of different online brokerages. Use Google.com or Yahoo.com to search for the names of the brokerages you are considering. You're sure to find some great message boards that will give you plenty of third-party opinions.

- *Go to the consumer advocates.* Just as there are watchdogs such as Consumer Reports that give us unbiased information about fridges and bicycles, so are there watchdogs of the financial industry. Kiplinger, Forrester, AAII and WatchFire GomezPro are all organizations that have amassed heap loads of surveys, data and statistics about online brokerages. For most of the really meaty information, you'll have to subscribe, but it's something you may want to consider. After all, we're talking about quite a bit of your money. A $50 subscription fee might be worth it for some solid facts.

The Deciding Factor

Still can't decide? This little tip is really, really trivial, and everything I told you about above is much more important when it comes to deciding on the right brokerage. But if you are so close to deciding that you need one last little tip to make up your mind, this may help. Call and ask for a sample statement. If it's clear, uses larger print, and makes you feel comfortable about what you're reading, that's your brokerage. It may seem like a relatively inconsequential deciding factor, but if you're really stuck, it can help break a tie.

Then What?

That's the easy part. Once you've decided on your brokerage, you'll want to start investing. Purchase a pre-made portfolio that matches your risk profile, or follow the instructions for choosing index funds in the "Do-It-Yourself Pocket Guide to Buying Mutual Funds Directly" on page 77.

To Recap:

- 401(k)s and IRAs are only for your retirement years. Once you've maxed them out, you'll have to find a new kind of account in which to place your investments.

- Once you pay off your debt you will have hundreds of extra dollars per month available to invest.

- A financial planner can help you OR

- You can go through a discount brokerage firm OR

- You can purchase directly OR

- You can go to a full-service brokerage firm.

- The easiest solution for the beginning investor is to invest in what are called index funds.

- There are many index funds to choose from, each managed by a different company.

- Regardless of the company that is managing the fund, all index funds that follow a particular index (i.e., S&P Index Funds) are fundamentally similar.

- Once you know which funds you want, call the mutual fund company that manages the fund and start buying! Or purchase through a broker. Or purchase through a financial planner.

ROUND EIGHT

TRACKING AND REBALANCING

Be you in what line of life you may, it will be amongst your misfortunes if you have not time properly to attend to pecuniary matters. Want of attention to these matters has impeded the progress of science and of genius itself. —William Cobbett

Congratulations! You have successfully created a diverse portfolio of investments. Now you may want to dash off and get back to your favorite hobby—gardening, tinkering with the car, cooking or whatever pleases you. But even though you may have more exciting things to do with your time, it doesn't mean you can just leave your investments unattended and hope they make good returns. You have to take an active role in maintaining your portfolio, tracking and rebalancing each year to keep up with changes in the market value of your investments. They say a watched pot never boils, but when it comes to your portfolio, you occasionally have to stir things up.

Wait, what does "Tracking and Rebalancing" mean?
Don't Let Your Money Spoil!

An overgrown garden doesn't give you juicy, ripe tomatoes and fat orange carrots. Neither do unwatched investments give you the best returns. While you aren't looking, the weighting of the allocated funds in your portfolio can change. Over the course of a year, funds in your portfolio will each earn a different return, some more, some less, which will change the balance in your portfolio.

It is also possible that your strategy or risk tolerance has changed, and by tracking and rebalancing you can readjust or weed out your asset allocations to match your most current needs. Otherwise, it could all boil over and you'll be left with less money in the pot than you had hoped for.

What is "Rebalancing?"
Mix it up. It's all in the wrist.

At the beginning of the fiscal year, you divide your money into different types of investments, just like you divide your vegetable garden into different rows of veggies. Remember your Risk Profile Quiz? You discovered your optimum portfolio allocation back in Round Five when you picked a risk profile based on your aversion to risk and the time you have until retirement. Each year you need to maintain your chosen risk profile.

Our buddy, Joe Average, will help us out by again providing an example.

Joe Average decides (for example's sake) to invest $100,000 dollars. According to his risk profile, Joe invests 60% of his money into Stock funds, and 40% into Bond funds.

Portfolio Asset Mix: Opening Balance

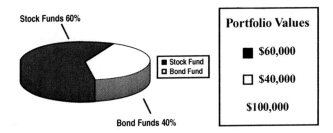

Joe's initial investment puts **$60,000** into stock funds and, **$40,000** into bond funds. One year goes by, and then Joe examines the returns earned by each fund. His equity funds performed much better than the bond funds, causing the percentage of his assets allocated towards stock funds to increase.

Portfolio Asset Mix: Year End Balance

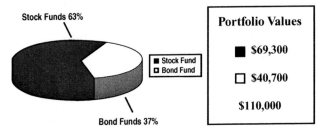

See how it's not equally divided anymore? His stock funds now account for more than **60%** of his assets, while his bond funds have dwindled to **37%**. If he wants to follow his original allocation mix strategy, he has to juggle his funds, selling off some of his stock funds and purchasing more bond funds. This will shift the balance back to his original percentages.

So, he reallocates his money, this time starting with **$110,000** (since his investments earned a healthy 10% rate of return) instead of **$100,000**. But he still wants to put **60% into Stocks, and 40% into Bonds.**

Portfolio Asset Mix: Ignored

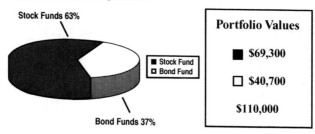

Portfolio Values

- ■ $69,300
- □ $40,700

$110,000

Portfolio Asset Mix: Rebalanced

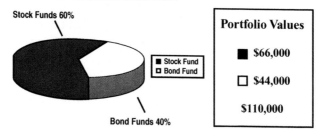

Portfolio Values

- ■ $66,000
- □ $44,000

$110,000

Now he's back on track. And he doesn't have to worry about taking more or less risk than his risk profile dictates.

What happens if I don't do anything and leave my portfolio alone?

The whole idea behind tracking and rebalancing is that you must maintain your appropriate allocation levels at all times, even if that means shifting stuff around. If you just "buy and hold" forever, you could wind up heavily weighted towards stocks. And the more you invest in stock funds, the more risk you are taking. YOU have direct control over your own level of risk. Don't leave things up to the Fickle Finger of Fate.

In order to maintain your personal ideal risk level, you must grab hold of the wheel and steer your portfolio back in the right direction. If a portfolio allocated at your appropriate risk level is "on the right track," a portfolio that weighs heavier on one or more funds is drifting off the road. Get back in your lane, buddy!

Sure, things could go differently and maybe in the second year, Joe's stock funds generate the strongest returns, in which case the unbalanced portfolio would make Joe more money than his rebalanced one. But that would require Joe to adhere to a more aggressive and riskier investment strategy, something he—or you—may not be comfortable doing. The opposite is also true, meaning that the stock fund could lose money—putting the bonds as prominent and then again, you are improperly allocated. The beauty of proper allocation and rebalancing is that over time it has been proven to reduce risk and smooth out returns.

> **Remember:** As you near retirement, you'll want to be shifting your investments toward the safety of treasury and fixed-income funds and away from the risk of stock funds, and you will need to rebalance your portfolio to minimize risk each year. In the post-Enron backlash, people are realizing that putting all of their retirement savings into company stock can be risky. Don't put all your eggs in one basket, no matter how sturdy and reliable you think that basket is. Stick to a sound financial principle by consistently diversifying, tracking, and rebalancing. Even if you have many years before retirement and lean towards a more aggressive portfolio, tracking and rebalancing are still necessary for you to keep your risk from spinning out of control.

I'm not saying your portfolio is heavy-maintenance. You don't have to feel like you are babysitting your portfolio, or holding hands with it year-round. However, tracking and rebalancing are wise practices with any investment strategy. You shouldn't plant the seeds of investment and not watch your money grow. To generate optimal results, investments must be nurtured and pruned like a well-kept garden.

**Ok, you've convinced me. But HOW do I
"Track and Rebalance?"**
It's easy as 1-2-3.

It only takes 3 simple steps to maintain the equilibrium of your portfolio. Though it may look easy to plant a seed, start a car, or whip up a chocolate cake, each takes specific steps to get the ideal result. And those steps all lead to wonderful results: a beautiful flower, a Sunday drive, or a delicious dish! What is the result when you invest carefully and properly? MORE MONEY!

Do-it-Yourself Example

Determine an annual or semiannual time for you to review the value of your portfolio and of each individual fund. It can be around your birthday, anniversary, the vernal equinox—whatever you choose— just select a consistent time each year that is convenient for you to do a little tinkering with your portfolio. Then, get to work.

If this is your Optimal Portfolio:

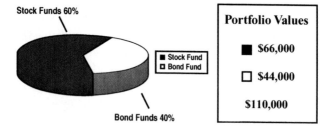

And this is what your Portfolio looks like now:

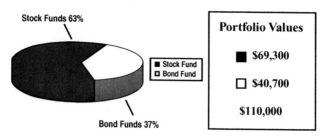

What should be the value of each of your funds after you rebalance?

Bond Fund_____

Stock Fund _____

Answer:

Looks complicated, but it's super simple. Just multiply your optimal percentage of each asset by your total current portfolio value, and you'll get your optimal value for each asset. So, optimal values are as follows:

Stock Fund Value: .60 X $110,000 = $66,000

Bond Fund Value: .40 X $110,000 = $44,000

In this example, that's the amount of money you should have invested in each asset to match your optimal portfolio.
See? Not so hard. It's your money, and you have the power to maintain an active role in its growth. You don't need to have a "green thumb" to grow your own money tree, just a little common sense and a calculator. Or, in cooking terms, when you enjoy a delicious dish you cooked yourself, the sense of accomplishment makes it taste all the better. Put some TLC into your portfolio to "sweeten the pot."

To Recap:

- As time goes by, the various funds in your portfolio will perform differently. A fund that performs particularly well (or particularly poorly) will shift the balance of your portfolio.

- If you leave your portfolio alone with its skewed weightings, you assume a different level of risk than your original strategy.

- You must rebalance your portfolio whenever a fund begins to outperform (or under perform) its optimal weight. Rebalance at least annually.

- As you get older, you will be reducing risk by increasing the ratio of bonds and decreasing the ratio of the riskier stock funds. Thus, your optimal portfolio will change over time.

ROUND NINE

THE FINISH LINE

If you can count your money, you don't have a billion dollars.
—*J. Paul Getty*

Whew! What a wild ride! You now know how to use your money wisely and to your advantage. Money no longer rules you. You rule it.

So that's it. You've reached the finish line. Now there's nothing to stand in your way of becoming a Reality Millionaire except a little determination and a healthy dose of willpower. Can't remember quite how you got here? On the next page is the pocket rulebook of Reality Millionaire, condensed, so you'll never miss a step.

REALITY MILLIONAIRE

The Game of Real Financial Life

POCKET RULEBOOK

For 1 Player & Family
Ages 18 to 118

SETUP: ROUND ONE

Start with a clean slate. Remove all current financial fears, worries and "can't do's" from your head. Discard them.

- Sign The Commitment (p. 4).
- Outline Your Dreams.
- Smile & Think Big.

RULES

Rule #1. The Golden Rule of Credit Card Use. Never charge more than you will pay off at the end of the month.

Rule #2. Once you make them, stick to your Debt Elimination Plan, Emergency Fund Plan and Investment Plans.

Rule #3. Never break Rule #1.

PLAY THE GAME

As you win and advance to each round of the game, you move on to doing bigger and better things with your money. You have to "win" each round to be able to move on to the next—and as you do, your bank account grows.

ROUNDS TWO & THREE:

The game starts by getting back to the starting line, debt-wise and security-wise.

a. Eliminate your debt by committing to a fixed monthly payment.

b. Map out where your dollars are headed each month. Direct your frivolous expenses to an Emergency Fund.

How to Win: Accumulate three months of living expenses in an Emergency Fund and stick to your Debt Elimination Plan until you are out of the red and back in black.

**Failing to maintain the Emergency Fund and Debt Elimination Plan indefinitely will result in being sent back to ROUND TWO and starting the game over again.

ROUNDS FOUR & FIVE:

Start choosing your investment types based on your risk profile. Will you play the game with a portfolio high in equity, or loaded with more secure assets like fixed-income or cash?

How to Win: Choose a portfolio that matches your risk profile, and move into round six with gusto.

ROUNDS SIX & SEVEN

Open a 401(k) or IRA and create an Investment Plan based on your risk profile. You may choose to hire a financial planner or broker to help you, or you may invest in funds directly yourself (Index funds are recommended).

Invest the same amount every month.

How to Win: Stick to your Investment Plan. You put hard work into creating this plan, now put it into action to reap the benefits.

*** Failing to maintain your Investment Plan indefinitely will result in losing massive amounts of money and not being able to retire on time.*

ROUND EIGHT

Rebalance your portfolio every year.

ROUND NINE
WINNING THE GAME

You've won the game when you've achieved the following:

• Security in the form of a three-month Emergency Fund.
• Freedom from debt.

• Enough money & investments to retire on.
• Enough money & investments to achieve your dreams set out in Round One.

KEEPING SCORE

To keep score, fill in the blanks below. Keep this pocketbook rule guide in your wallet. Carry it wherever you go. Whenever you feel like you might break a rule, refer to the numbers below. As you achieve each goal, check them off.

I will deposit $_____ into my Emergency Fund every month until I reach a total of $_____.

I have a full Emergency Fund.

I will make a fixed payment of $_____ to my debtors every month (as well as pay off any new monthly debt in full).

I have paid off my debt.

I will deposit $_____ into my investments every month until I am ready to retire.

I have enough money to retire.

I have enough money to feel financially free. I'll never worry, "Where's the money's coming from?" again.

I have won Reality Millionaire!

You hold the key to your future. Believe me, I know. Just 15 years ago, I was Joe Average—living paycheck to paycheck, panicking each month when the bills came in, debt up to my ears, and with no light at the end of what looked like a long, long tunnel. I was thousands of dollars in debt. How do you get out of a hole like that? It's actually not as hard as people might think.

All it takes is a simple commitment to follow the basic steps of debt management and investments. Reality Millionaire is a game anyone can win. You are already playing Reality Millionaire; you have been in the game since you saved your first nickel, opened your first bank account or accepted your first credit card. But most people never learned to read the rulebook. Now you have, and now you have the secrets to winning it all!

Good luck!

What follows is some supplemental material I've provided to aid you in the game of Reality Millionaire.

RETIREMENT
PLANNING TUTORIAL

SAVE SOME GREENBACKS
SO YOU CAN ENJOY THE GREENS ON THE BACK NINE

Up until now, we have been steadily working through your finances and keeping them in order. You know how much you owe, how much you spend, and how much you have. Now it is time to think about how much you are going to need many years down the road when you retire from this crazy rat race.

This chapter is only a tutorial, because retirement planning can involve a great deal of complex factors such as stock market cycles, inflation data, cost of living index, and more. All of those terms may sound intimidating, but you don't have to worry about that. Professional retirement planners or retirement planning software can help you get a handle on those aspects. Your life will be in a constant flux, and your retirement plans may change over the years. But this chapter can explain how you can start thinking about the future today and what you can do NOW to help yourself live more comfortably later.

Retirement planning is all about numbers and preparation (don't wince, it'll be fine). You need to collect all these numbers and plot out your retirement course, learning to avoid life's sand traps and water hazards along the way.

Retirement
Par for the Course of Life

It may seem that retirement is so far off in the future that it's not even worth trying to plan for. There are so many unknowns that you can't possibly plan ahead, so why bother?

Actually, if you want to retire in true comfort and financial security, the sooner you start planning, the better. The U.S. Department of Labor reports that for every 10 years you delay in saving for retirement, you'll have to save three times more each month to catch up.

What does it mean to retire?

Well, it means you get to stop working and that you get to enjoy every hour of every day doing what you want to do, whether that's traveling, gardening, shopping or golfing. But it also means that you stop getting a regular paycheck, so "retirement planning" means planning how you are going to have enough money to live on once the paychecks stop coming in.

Plotting The Course
From Your First Swing to Relaxing at the Clubhouse

Retirement planning is a combination of calculating what you will have and what you will need, and then trying to make the numbers match up.

So, we'll use a simple method to keep score and get some ballpark figures. But, before we tally up the dollar amount you need to win the game, we need to know the basic numbers we'll be dealing with. It may look math-heavy, but I'll try to make it as painless as possible.

To know how much you'll need to invest every month towards retirement, you'll need to know the following numbers:

- How much annual income you want to retire on
- How many years from now you plan to retire
- How many years you will live on retirement
- The rate of inflation
- The rate of interest you expect to earn from your investments
- Your monthly Social Security benefits

Don't have a clue yet as to what these numbers are? Don't worry. The following sections will help you figure them out.

How much annual income do you want to retire on?

Once you retire, you will still have a sort of income, called your "Retirement Income." That is the amount of money you will live on each year of your retirement. This "Retirement Income" comes from your savings and return from investments. You are essentially paying yourself out of your own bank account, but consider it the same as your usual yearly income.

How do you decide how much you will need?

Basic Income: Examine your current expenses. You will need to consider changing needs. You won't need to commute to work anymore, and you won't need to spend money on work clothes. But what else will you need instead? Medications, more comfortable shoes, a different diet, or other expenses may pop up.

You'll also want to consider who else you might be supporting. Will you still have kids in college? Will you be taking care of one or both of your elderly parents? When you retire, you could still be responsible for more people than just you and your spouse. And don't forget your pets. One of your goals may be breeding champion sheepdogs, or high-demand hamsters.

Your target retirement income may be the same as your annual income now, or you may decide you need a couple thousand dollars less.

If you have been playing Reality Millionaire and sticking to your Debt Elimination Plan, by the time you retire from the daily grind, you will have eliminated most of your heavier debts. Your mortgage will likely be paid off by then, freeing up thousands of dollars a year for you to live on. College loans will be paid off. You will reduce some of the smaller expenses that chipped away at your income—gas and lunch on the go, for example.

Because of the reduction in your cost of living after retirement, most financial planners recommend that you will only need about 70%–80% of your current family income. You may want to figure your retirement this way or you might want to figure it at 100% of your current income to be on the safe side.

Based on your current income and budget, write down an estimated figure that will represent your "Basic Retirement Income":_____.

First, make sure you can achieve this basic goal, and then focus on the "Fun Budget." You don't need an RV, but you might need an IV.

Fun Income: What do you want to do when you retire? Buy an RV and travel the country. Move to Florida and spend your days on the beach. Open up a little antiques store. Or spend every other day at the links. What do you plan on doing once you are on permanent vacation? Jot down a list of a just a few ideas you might be tossing around, just for fun:

_____

_____

_____

_____

How much money will you need to do these things?

So, now that you have some idea of what you will be doing, you can start to imagine what it is going to cost you. For example:

Buy an RV: $90,000
Buy a rustic cabin in the mountains: $150,000
Buy a new set of golf clubs: $600

Choose a number that represents your "Retirement Fun Budget" each year. Record that number here: _____.

Target Retirement Income: To find out your total target retirement income, add up the numbers you wrote down for your basic annual retirement income and your fun annual retirement income.

My Target Annual Retirement Income is:_____.

For the purpose of our tutorial, I am going to work with the Target Retirement Income of $45,000 annually, total. But if you wish to follow along using your own number, feel free to work right along with me. We'll go step by step.

When do you want to retire?

Wouldn't it be fun to be able to retire early, as early as age 55, and have almost the whole second half of your life left to do what you really want? When you start planning, you have to decide when you want to retire. If you want to retire early, you are going to have to put extra work into preparing so that when the time comes, you are ready. If you plan to retire at the usual age, 65, you still have work to do, but you have an extra decade to do it. The choice is yours, but try to decide now, because it effects what you do during the time between now and then.

I want to retire in _____ years.

How long will you be living on retirement?

If you plan to retire at 65, you should realistically plan to live another 15–20 years. With advancements in health sciences, by 2030, our life expectancy will most likely have risen to 80 years of age or older. That's over a decade and a half or more past retirement age. You'll have to plan to make your retirement savings last at least that long, just to be safe.

The United States ranks 17th in average life expectancy on a list of 33 developed nations according to a report from the U.S. Centers for Disease Control in 2005. Japan comes in at #1 with an average life expectancy of 79.1 years.

I plan to live for _____ years in retirement.

You now have three of the numbers that you need for your retirement planning:

- How much annual income you want to retire on
- How many years from now you plan to retire
- How many years you will live in retirement

Now, most likely, your first instinct to finding out how much total money you'll need to save for retirement is to do something like this. . . .

Target Retirement Savings	=	Annual Retirement Income	x	Number of Years in Retirement

_____ **Target Retirement Savings**

_____ **Amount to Save Each Year Toward Retirement**

_____ **Number of Years Until Retirement**

So, for example, if you plan to retire on $45,000 for 20 years and you have 25 years to save, it seems natural that you would do the following calculation:

Target Retirement Savings = $45,000 X 20 = $900,000

Amount to Save Each Year Toward Retirement = $900,000 / 25 = $36,000

Thank goodness that's not the right number, or you would have to save over $3,000 a month towards retirement!

There are two other major factors that will affect your retirement planning: inflation and investments.

How will inflation affect my plans?

Remember when candy bars cost 25 cents and a quart of milk was less than a dollar? We have inflation to thank for the wildly different prices we pay now. The estimated rate of inflation is between 2% and 5%. But what does that mean?

$45,000 now will not mean the same thing as $45,000 in 25 years, or even 10 years. In 25 years, in order to get the same standard of living you currently get out of $45,000, you have to apply the rate of inflation to the figure. If you are working along with me, break out your calculator.

Rate of Growth or Inflation

	2%	3%	4%	5%
5 years	1.10	1.16	1.22	1.28
10 years	1.22	1.34	1.48	1.63
15 years	1.35	1.56	1.80	2.08
20 years	1.49	1.81	2.19	2.65
25 years	1.64	**2.09**	2.67	3.39
30 years	1.81	2.43	3.24	4.32
35 years	—	2.81	3.95	5.52
40 years	—	3.26	4.80	7.04

Soooo, what do we do with that chart and all those numbers? We have decided that we are going to retire at $45,000 a year, but we understand that we have to figure out what "$45,000" actually translates to in the future. To do so, we select the number of years until we retire, then we choose a predicted annual rate of inflation. Here, we will be careful and predict 3%. And we plan to retire in 25 years.

Therefore, to calculate how much money we'll need if you want to retire on today's $45,000 lifestyle, we select the annual rate of inflation from the chart and multiply it by our desired Retirement Income ($45,000 or whatever you wish):

$45,000 X 2.09 = $94,050 annual retirement living expenses in 25 years

If you are working with your own number: _____

See what I mean? You can't just say, "I want to retire on $45,000 a year," and multiply it times however many years you'll be on retirement, because if you did that, you'd have a wildly inaccurate number. That'd be like if 20 years ago you planned to buy 20 candy bars in 2007, and you opened a savings account to start saving. At the time you started saving, candy bars only cost $.25. If you didn't allow for inflation, you'd wind up with a whopping $5. Candy bars actually went up in price to $1.00, so by the time you got to your account the $5 will only buy you five candy bars, not 20 . . . oops! And that's not including tax!

But inflation doesn't end the minute you retire; it continues to affect your money year after year. If the rate of inflation is 3%, then your money in the bank is worth 3% less each year that goes by. That means, each year, in order to live the EXACT same way you lived the year before, you'd have withdrawn 3% more from your bank account.

Fortunately, your income will probably be adjusted for inflation by your employer, so as long as you are working and saving, you won't wind up falling behind the times.

I know, I know, the math is getting overwhelming. Hang on.

Let's review quickly:

• Inflation will make your money worth less and less each year that goes by.

• Your annual living expenses will also, of course, deplete your savings each year.

But there's good news, too!

Investments and Interest to the Rescue!

• The interest and return you earn on your investments will actually add to your bank account each year—before and during your retirement

But what about Social Security?

Social Security, while not as secure as we may hope, does contribute to your retirement savings, reducing the amount you have to save. To calculate your Social Security benefits in "future" dollars, visit the Social Security Web site at www.ssa.gov. For the purpose of our example, we will have an estimated monthly benefit of $2,864. I would like to point out that, historically, the government does not return as much as the return on your own money.

We have calculated that in 25 years, at a 3% inflation rate, Joe will need $94,050 annually in his retirement years. That translates to $7,837 per month. We then subtract his expected Social Security benefits. Joe will only need $4,973 in living expenses per month, when you account for Social Security. Remember, this is in future dollars. We have applied the rate of inflation over the next 25 years to see the future equivalent of today's dollars.

So how do you take all of this into account?

Now you're ready to swing for that oh-so-much-greener grass, and you don't have to be a prophet to estimate your profit. To get a rough idea of how much you'll need, follow these steps:

Step 1. To estimate the amount you'll need to withdraw each year from your retirement account, we are going to do the calculation from the "How Will Inflation Affect My Plans?" section

Step 2. Calculate your annual Social Security benefits by figuring your monthly Social Security benefits and multiplying them by twelve. (You can estimate your monthly Social Security benefits using the calculator at www.ssa.gov.)

Step 3. Calculate the total money you will need in retirement by subtracting Step 2 from Step 1 and multiplying the answer by the number of years you will be in retirement

Step 4. Now, to find how much you need to save each month to get to the number in Step 3, you have to take into account how well your investments will do before retirement. That is, the better your investments do, the less you'll have to put away every month to reach your goal. The easiest way to calculate how much you'll need to save is by using a savings calculator. Visit www.realitymillionaire.com for the official Reality Millionaire savings calculator.

Step 5. Don't Panic.

EXAMPLE

Joe Average wants to retire on $45,000. He believes the rate of inflation will be 3%, and he plans to retire in 25 years. He uses the chart from the "How Will Inflation Affect My Plans?" section to calculate his annual living expenses in retirement:

$$\$45,000 \text{ X } 2.09 = \$94,050$$

Joe uses the Social Security calculator to calculate his future monthly benefits. Based on his current income and retirement date, he discovers he will be making **$2,864** in Social Security benefits every month (future dollars). To calculate how much Social Security he will receive annually during retirement, he multiplies this by 12:

$2,864 X 12 = $34,368

Joe wants to spend 20 years in retirement. To find how much total money he will need to withdraw over his retirement, he calculates: (1) The total amount needed to live in retirement each year minus social security received each year, and then (2) multiplies that figure by the total number of years he plans to spend in retirement:

Step 1) $94,050 - $34,368 = $59,682

Step 2) $59,682 X 20 = $1,193,640*

*This is the total amount of money that Joe will spend in retirement, above and beyond his Social Security benefits.

Joe uses his favorite savings calculator to calculate how much he'll need to save every month to meet this goal if his investments earn a 10% rate of return and he saves for 25 years.

The calculator tells him he'll need to save roughly $928.00 every month.

Did you say $928?? What happened to becoming a millionaire by saving just a couple hundred bucks? Ah, but if you remember, we also talked about getting out of debt. And if your debt payment is anything like Joe Average's you are probably paying close to $1480 per month to your creditors. Once they are paid off, there's your nest egg! So, you see, you have the money already. It's just going into the wrong pocket right now—your creditor's. As soon as you get out of debt, you can be spending that money on investments for the future. Plus, with your employer likely matching your 401(k) investments, and an annual increase in your salary, you'll have even more "extra" money to work with!

Just for kicks, I am going to give you an example that demonstrates how beneficial it is to start early. It really does make a difference.

Imagine you are only 10 years away from retiring instead of 30. At www.realitymillionaire.com you can use the savings calculator and you'll find that you need to save a whopping $69,924 (figuring a 10% return) annually for the next ten years. That's $5,827 a month that you would need to save for retirement! Doesn't $928 a month sound a whole lot better? There's a reason early tee times are so popular! The more time you have, the better.

One Last Stop Before We Look at the Score Cards

If you've been following closely, you may have noticed that we actually made one big assumption. We assumed that after retirement, the only factor affecting the balance in your retirement account would be your annual withdrawals for living expenses (your annual retirement income). But that's not true. You see, inflation and return on investments will both continue to affect your savings after you've retired.

To avoid this extra calculation, for our purposes we assumed that, after retirement, your return on investments and the rate of inflation will cancel each other out. In fact, you might make more than enough to keep up with inflation. But we made this assumption to simplify the explanation. This isn't an unsafe assumption. If you remember Round Five, you'll recall that the closer you are to retirement, the more safe, fixed-income investments you'll include in your portfolio. These safer investments will also yield a lower rate of return, close to the rate of inflation at 2% to 5%.

Of course, it's also important to understand that this is an assumption, and that after retirement your bank account is not actually static, but will continue to be affected by positive and negative factors:

A) Positive Factors: Interest, Return on Investment
B) Negative Factors: Inflation, Annual Withdrawals

> • If **A is less than B,** you will have less money in your account year after year of retirement.

> • If **A is greater than B**, you will have more money in your account, year after year.

By now you see how complicated Retirement Planning can get, but you have also gained a basic understanding of the factors that will affect how much you plan to save and how you plan to live on the money you have when you retire. You also see that having income from interest and investment is vital in keeping your account healthy enough to be able to continue on the same standard of living, year after year of retirement.

Now, all of this can change. No one can be certain what the rate of inflation will be. You can't be certain how your investments will pay off. You cannot even be sure what your own expected annual expenses will be, because medical expenses or other emergencies or even basic lifestyle changes can pop up at anytime. Nobody can be 100% accurate when predicting your future. But a professional retirement planner or commercially available retirement planning software can try to give you an idea of what's in store. Having some basic idea of what's next is better than careening helter-skelter into the future.

OH MY GOSH, what do I do if I haven't done anything yet?!

Remain calm. The worst thing you can do is panic and start throwing your money into risky investments, hoping desperately that you can suddenly make up for lost time. But fear not, because hope is not lost. You'll need to take some serious action to achieve a comfortable retirement nest egg, but you can do it. The reality of it is: you've got some hard work ahead of you, but avoiding it won't make it any easier.

Last Minute Retirement Planning

Ideally, you have been putting away 10% of your income every year since your very first job out of college. Ideally, you have set up a 401(k) with your current employer, or have been investing in an IRA. Ideally, you have a diverse portfolio of stocks and bonds that will grant you a huge Return On Investment. Ideally, you happen to be holding a winning lottery ticket in your hand. But things aren't always ideal.

Address Your Uncertainty Head On
Keep Your Head Down, Take a Deep Breath, and Swing

You are armed with enough information to start planning right now, no matter how soon you'll be retiring. Nobody ever thinks they are well enough prepared when they start turning the numbers around in their head. Don't just shrug and say, "It's no use; I'm too late."

Jump Into Action

Time to start putting money away now. Load up on your tax-deductible retirement funds. Put as much money as you can into the 401(k) or IRA. Those alone can help you increase your retirement funds substantially due to the preferable tax status of these accounts. But you can do more. Start making some money off of your savings, by investing wisely in a diversified portfolio. Continue to invest during your retirement in order to create a continuing income, to help you keep up with the rate of inflation. You can put your money to work while you sit back and enjoy your retirement.

Where are you going to get the money to pay off your mortgage if you are throwing all your weight into your 401(k) or IRA? There are two ways to step up the savings and make your dough rise.

Increase Your Income

You can find ways to make a few extra dollars a week by starting a business on the side or turning a hobby into an income. See the following section, "Sources of Extra Income," for ideas. Remember, you don't have to just sit around the minute you turn 65. People who work longer live longer. You can choose to postpone your retirement, or you can retire from one career and do something else that interests you. Retirement is your time to do what you want—and if you can make some extra money while you are at it, all the better.

Decrease Your Expenses

In Round Two, we found a way to squeeze about 10% of your income out of your expenses. By cutting down on just one or two expensive habits, you can save hundreds of dollars. The more you cut, the more you save. Some retirement planning specialists recommend you put the equivalent of one hour's worth of your daily income into retirement savings. At $45,000 a year, that works out to about $21 dollars an hour, so you should attempt to save $21 a day towards that glorious day when you retire. Even if you are able to just save $10 a day, assuming a 10% return, you could have $233,000 in 20 years.

Where can you find $10 a day? Read the paper online instead of having it delivered to your door. Have a banana for breakfast instead of a donut or fast-food treat. Drink water instead of soda. Carpool. Take a brown bag lunch to work. Rent a movie instead of springing for tickets. You can chip away at your daily expenses with very little pain. Would you really miss that donut each morning? Years from now, when you are enjoying your retirement years worry-free, drinking cool lemonade in the clubhouse, you'll be glad you put a little extra effort into retirement planning.

How can you tell if you are on the right track? How do you know if you are doing enough to be ready? A professional retirement or financial planner can help you calculate the sort of numbers you'll be working with (see my section on Choosing a Financial Planner). There may be many years between now and then, and things can change, so always check the rate of your progress every year against any lifestyle changes and make adjustments accordingly.

You can't just decide you need "X" amount of dollars to retire, then save, save, save and expect to arrive at age 65 perfectly prepared to live out the rest of your years in financial comfort. It takes some planning and effort to understand the true complexities of retirement finances.

As you can see, there are a number of factors you must consider when it comes to retirement planning. Not to mention wills, estate planning, medical bills, possible nursing home care, or any number of other unpleasant issues that must be dealt with as you get older. I should mention that the scenario we have presented does not generally leave anything for your heirs, other than your house and any life insurance. Regardless of all that, remember, the span of your retirement is known as Your Golden Years. You will have earned them and have the right to enjoy them any way you wish.

Retirement Planning boils down to this:

Don't panic. Know how much money you want to retire with, and then focus on making sure you have it when the time comes.

SOURCES OF EXTRA INCOME

HOW TO MAKE YOUR DOUGH RISE QUICKLY

Throughout this book, I have discussed ways you can get out of debt, stay out of debt, save money, and make money through wise investments. But maybe you are looking for a more active way to make some extra cash. Or maybe you need some immediate dough. Whatever your needs, here are a few ways to have a little more money in your piggy bank.

Turn A Hobby Into An Income
Craft Shows, Catering, Photography, Babysitting . . .

Could you be making extra money just doing the things you love? Chances are, you can find a way to turn your free time into extra moolah, no matter what your hobby is. If you enjoy woodwork, sell some of your handcrafted rocking chairs. Craft shows are inexpensive and easy markets to sell any of your wares, from quilts to canned peaches.

Speaking of canned peaches, if your favorite pastime is cooking, and your friends are always raving about your culinary creations, why not offer to cater their next party? You can explore all sorts of exotic and interesting recipes, while making extra "dough."

Maybe your children are grown up and you miss the pitter-patter of little feet. You can offer your babysitting services around your neighborhood. Parents with young children will pay almost anything to get a night out on their own. Don't you remember what that was like?

Just set the wheels of creativity in motion and you could probably think of a way to turn any hobby into an extra source of income— and you'll have extra fun!

A recent AARP survey showed that 68% of working people over the age of 50 plan to work for pay even after they retire from their current careers. Plus, more than three-quarters of those surveyed said they expected to keep working in some form, simply because they enjoyed it, not for the money. So you can work doing something you truly enjoy, and get both money and a sense of achievement out of your job, no matter what it is.

Utilize Your Strengths and Resources
It May Not Be Your Hobby, But Maybe It's Your Hidden Talent

Ask yourself: "What am I really good at?" If you have an unusual talent for doing something others might consider a chore, you might be able to earn yourself some money just by doing something you are good at. You don't have to charge your friends for doing them such a favor, but if you tell them to let their friends know about you, and then those people tell their friends, word will get out and you can start having your own little niche business.

Consider these questions to discover an untapped source of income for yourself:

Are you a neatnik?

Is your home perfectly organized and spotless? Next time a friend compliments you on your clutter-free home and laments that theirs isn't so tidy, you can offer to help them get organized. Word could get around that you are a master at organizing an overcrowded garage, and you could find yourself with a steady income!

Are you a computer whiz?

If you know computers inside out, you can offer to help your neighbors whenever they run into a problem. Soon you will be the local Computer Guy (or Gal) and pick up some quick cash just helping someone install new software.

Are you a bargain hound?

If you know how to hunt down the best price on anything, you can tutor others to have a nose for a good deal as well. Or you could be a personal shopper, and shop for others while shopping for yourself at the same time!

Are you a style guru?

You can cut your neighbor's kids' hair for a fraction of the price they would pay at a barbershop. Or you can do your friend's daughter's hair for her prom. If beauty is your thing, help make the world a more beautiful place, one person at a time—for a small fee.

Do you have a green thumb?

Sell your homegrown tomatoes and cucumbers—after you have gotten your fill of them first, of course. People love fresh, home-grown produce. Wrap it all up in pretty bags or baskets and take your produce to work or to a local community center the same time each week and people will begin to depend on you for their fresh bell peppers!

Are you clever in the kitchen?

You can do the same for baked goods, as well. Nice presentation is key, as is consistency. You can turn boring old Tuesdays into Cookie Day at work and make enough money to go out to the movies on Friday!

Do you own a large van or truck?

If you don't mind helping with some heavy lifting, you can help people move a few items of furniture. Just be sure to lift with your legs.

Do you have a spare room or garage apartment?

Especially if you live near a college campus, you can have a solid income for a set period of time by renting out your spare bedroom or garage apartment. You have to be sure to select a trustworthy boarder, and your family must be prepared to get used to some changes, but renting out space is an excellent way to have steady money coming in each month. College students are great customers—they're willing to live in a small amount of space, and you can rent by the semester or over the summer.

Some Simple Ways to Make Extra Money: Think Like a Kid Again

- Mow lawns
- Rake leaves
- Shovel driveways
- Walk dogs
- Bathe dogs
- Clean swimming pools

- Water plants
- Weed flower beds and gardens
- Run errands (while running your own errands!)
- Wash cars
- Address wedding invitations
- Mend or alter clothes
- Provide photography or videography services at parties

Simplify Your Life
One Man's Trash. . . .

Have a Garage Sale

You'll make a few hundred dollars by getting rid of the junk you have accumulated over the decades. Make sure your children don't want it before you sell it, though. Clutter to you could be a cherished memory to them. They may be secretly in love with the lamp decorated with seashells that you got 30 years ago on a trip to the Florida Keys. You never know.

Sell it on Ebay

People have made whole careers out of buying and selling items on online auction sites. You may have an old children's book that some desperate collector is willing to pay top dollar for. Use a regular garage sale to get rid of basic items, but if you have anything truly unique, try putting it up for sale at an auction site like Ebay. You may be totally surprised by how much you get for it!

Put Clothes on Consignment

If you have no need for your old prom dress or that powder blue tuxedo you'll never wear again, consignment is a great way to open up some space in your closet and get some money for it. When you sell something by consignment, it means the consignment store takes a percentage of the money, but it is a great outlet for selling clothing items that are in good condition. You'll actually make more money selling such items on consignment than at a garage sale. But don't try to sell a 15-year-old tracksuit. That's garage sale material, my friend.

Move to an Affordable Paradise
Move from Manhattan to Montauk and Live Happily for Less

This may be a little drastic, but if you find yourself really struggling for money, consider this: You might be living in an expensive city. The cost of living varies wildly across the United States. In fact, it can vary wildly within the city limits! In Houston, Texas, $20,000 can pay a year's rent on a tiny two-bedroom apartment downtown, or it can be the down payment and half the mortgage on a three-bedroom house in an older neighborhood just a few miles away.

Some parts of the country are just plain cheaper to live in. For example, Forbes Magazine reports that you can satisfy your need for big-city drama on a small-town budget by moving just 90 minutes north of pricey San Francisco to sophisticated Santa Rosa, California. To find urban living for a bargain, look

Average City U.S.A	100
Anchorage, Alaska	109
Phoenix, Arizona	57
Little Rock, Arkansas	68
Los Angeles, California	133
San Francisco, California	217
Boulder, Colorado	121
Denver, Colorado	135
Hartford, Connecticut	111
Stamford, Connecticut	160
Atlanta, Georgia	115
Chicago, Illinois	166
Louisville, Kentucky	79
New Orleans, Louisiana	89
Baltimore, Maryland	103
Boston, Massachusetts	240
Detroit, Michigan	98
Minneapolis, Minnesota	88
Omaha, Nebraska	106
Las Vegas, Nevada	80
Albuquerque, New Mexico	82
Buffalo, New York	77
New York City, New York	364
Cleveland, Ohio	93
Oklahoma City, Oklahoma	61
Austin, Texas	93
Salt Lake City, Utah	99
Alexandria, Virginia	143
Seattle, Washington	108
Washington, D.C.	181
Madison, Wisconsin	101

for a rapidly growing city with plenty of extra housing, and you can snap up something at half the price of dwellings in more established metropolises like Chicago or Boston.

The Cost of Living Index is an easy way to figure out in which cities your money will go the farthest. Don't worry, there's a simple little equation to compare. The University of Notre Dame publishes a list of the Cost of Living index for 87 popular towns and cities in the United States. On the left is a list of the top Cost of Living index in a random 30 cities.

So, say you wanted to know how far your $30,000 a year salary would get you in Austin as opposed to Boston. Divide the indexes of the two cities, highest by the lowest, and multiply it by your salary.

Boston (240) divided by Austin (93) times salary ($30,000) = $77,419. Wow! Uh, what does that mean? It means that you will live more than twice as well on the same amount of money in Austin as you would in Boston! Movie tickets, dining out, housing . . . it is all cheaper in Austin. Where would you rather live?

Of course, this doesn't mean you have to pick up and move your life halfway across the country. I just wanted to point out that even moving a few miles out of town could save you a few hundred (or thousand) dollars. And, if you do want to move someplace new, it's a good idea to check the cost of living there, just to see how it measures up.

Look Under The Couch Cushions
And Under the Seats of Your Car, Too

You won't find wads of cash, of course. But you'll surely find some loose change! The message is to get up and look around, because you may be sitting on money without even knowing it. It only takes a little effort and creative thinking to line your pockets with a few more dollars. And remember, if you found just $1 extra per day, you'd make an extra $365 a year!

CREDIT 101

UNDERSTANDING YOUR CREDIT SCORE

You may or may not know it, but even though school is over, you are still being graded. How? Your credit score. Your credit score can determine whether or not you get a job, a bank loan, even a home or apartment. So it is vital that you understand not only what your score is and why, but how you can improve your score. Who wouldn't want to do some extra credit (no pun intended) to go from a C to an A+?

Let's begin. Don't raise your hand if you have a question. Just read on.

What is a Credit Score?

To put it simply, a credit score is a grade on a report card for grown-ups. It is based on your credit behavior: whether you pay your bills on time, whether you pay off loans, how much debt you are in, and so on. In short, it rates how responsible you are with your money. You want a high credit score, because it shows you pay your bills on time and can be trusted to pay back loans or any incurred debt.

133

Why is my Credit Score important?

Say a buddy asks you to spot him some dough because he is short on rent this month. You know he is notoriously bad about paying people back. How likely are you to fork over the cash? You risk the chance of never seeing that money again.

Your credit score is an assessment of a similar risk. Are you likely to pay back that loan you are asking for? Are you going to pay your rent on time? Your credit score isn't a fortune-teller. It can't say for sure whether or not you are a good customer or a bad customer. But it can use past patterns of behavior to predict your future actions when it comes to your financial responsibility.

Reviewing your credit score is a sort of background check, used by anyone who needs to know how much of a financial risk you are. Usually, credit scores are used to determine interest rates on mortgages, and cars etc. However, your credit score is also being evaluated by banks, employers, landlords, credit card companies, even utility companies. A very low credit score could leave you sitting in the dark.

But what determines my specific numerical score?

Your credit score is calculated based on statistical data and objective evaluations of your past behavior. You are awarded or lose points for various factors. Bill payment history, amounts owed, length of credit history, new credit, and types of credit used: all of these factors are gathered by the credit reporting agencies. Then they compare all of your credit information against the statistics of people with similar profiles and add up your points based on those factors. The total number of points determines how reliable you are.

The percentages in the following graph represent the importance of each category in determining the score for the general population.

Let's examine each of these factors in a bit more detail.

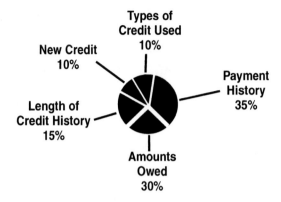

Payment History—Your payment history is the most significant, of course, because lenders want to know how likely you will be to make your payments on time and in full.

Amounts Owed—Lenders want to know how much outstanding debt you have. High balances will lower your score.

Length of Credit History—If you have a short credit history, you haven't had time to establish an accurate depiction of your credit behavior. The less accurate your credit history, the lower your overall score.

New Credit—If you have applied for several new credit accounts or loans in the past year, those inquiries will appear on your report. It may appear that you are having a financial emergency or are in a great deal of debt, which will have a negative effect on your score.

Types of Credit Used—Though there is no ideal combination of loans and credit cards, it's generally a good idea to have some revolving debt (i.e., credit cards) and some fixed-payment debt (i.e., loans). The kinds of debt you currently have are taken into consideration, especially if you have a short credit history and other factors are less accurate.

Keep in mind that the credit reporting agencies have different modes of evaluation. Some place more significance on certain factors, and less on others, but your credit score is generally going to fall in the same range at each agency, no matter what method of assessment. Banks and other lenders can use this score to assess the risk of lending money to you, or leasing an apartment to you, or even giving you a job. Obviously, you want a good score.

Other Tidbits to Note:

- All of these factors are considered as a whole.

- These percentages are for the general population. The importance of these factors varies from person to person.

- Your credit score takes only these factors into account, but individual lenders may look at additional factors such as your income or how long you have held your current job.

- You lose points on your score for negative information, but you also gain points on your score for positive information, such as starting to make payments on time after having a bad track record for being late.

So, what's a good credit score?

We have spent a long time talking about why you need to have a good credit score, so you can enjoy lowered interest rates on credit cards and mortgages. But just what is a "good credit score." Time to whip out the Credit Score Report Card.

If you rank in C or below, you will most surely be forced to pay higher interest rates, simply due to your poor credit score.

760 or Above	**A⁺**
700–760	**A**
650–700	**B**
600–650	**C**
550–600	**D**
Below 550	**F**

Is my credit score permanent?

You are not going to be stuck with the same credit score forever. There is not going to be a giant "619" branded on your forehead for the rest of your life. Your credit score can change just as much as your GPA did in school. Remember sophomore year of school? Yeah, that wasn't such a great year. But you holed yourself up in the library and by graduation you were Cum Laude.

So goes your credit score. It is just a snapshot of your current financial situation. It can fluctuate based on whether you pay your bills on time or a few days late, get a new credit card account, or take out a new loan. You may have a high credit score until one month you simultaneously forget to pay the mortgage and have to use your credit card to pay for $5,000 worth of damage to your car, thanks to your teenage son. Or, you may start off with a low credit score but build it up slowly over time, paying off debts, paying bills on time, and wisely using the credit cards. The longer you maintain on-time payments, the higher your credit score will climb.

Pop Quiz!

Q: Is a low credit score good or bad?

A: Bad.

I don't even know my credit score, how do I find out?

There are three main credit-reporting agencies in the United States, and most lenders get your credit score from one of The Big Three.

• Equifax: (800) 685-1111
• Experian (formerly TRW): (888) EXPERIAN (397-3742)
• Trans Union: (800) 916-8800

Thanks to The Fair And Accurate Credit Transactions Act, which passed December 1, 2004, and is now in effect all over the U.S., each American consumer is entitled to a free yearly review of their credit report. You may request this yearly review from any one of the Big Three mentioned above. You may opt to add your credit score to your free credit report for a minimal charge.

If at some other point during the year you would like to check up on your credit report, you can request a copy for a small fee, ranging from $10 to $40 dollars.

Your score may vary from agency to agency. Though they use similar evaluation method software, their methods of evaluation can result in a discrepancy in scores. They could have different information on you, or be comparing you to a different statistical pool. Both Equifax and Trans Union currently use FICO methods. Experian has implemented their own proprietary method—the others may follow suit at some point.

There's a quicker way to getting your free credit report. To make it more convenient to get your annual checkup, the Big Three have teamed up.

• **Call toll-free** at (877) 322-8228
• **Go online** to www.annualcreditreport.com
• **Or request by mail** at *Annual Credit Report Request Service, P.O. Box 105281, Atlanta, GA 30348-5281*

Note: You may hear your credit report referred to as a "FICO score." This is because the main three credit reporting agencies once used the same software to determine most scores, software developed by Fair Isaac and Company. Now the term has become standard, even if the actual FICO software isn't used to calculate the score.

Other Names for Credit Scores

Credit scores have different names at each of the three credit reporting agencies. All of these scores, however, are developed using similar methods, and have been rigorously tested to ensure they provide the most accurate picture of credit risk possible using credit report data.

Credit Reporting Agency	Credit Score
Equifax	BEACON®
Experian	VantageScore$_{SM}$
TransUnion	EMPIRICA®

Pop Quiz!

Q: Is your credit score permanent?

A: No

I know my credit score, and I want to improve it. How?

Now you see how important your credit score is. If you are turned down for a loan or denied credit based on a low credit score, it is your right to know what is causing your low credit score. Your creditor may tell you that you have some outstanding bank loans or a balance that is too close to your limit. Once you know which factors are a "black mark" on your score, you can go about eliminating those factors and raising your score. Then you can reapply for that loan or credit card.

The number one way to have a good credit score is to pay all your bills—ON TIME. Don't let anything slide. Be responsible and trustworthy with all finances, and your score will make your mama proud.

How do I know my credit score is fair?

The Equal Credit Opportunity Act stipulates that characteristics such as race, sex, ethnicity, and religion cannot be used as factors in determining a credit score.

What is the difference between a credit report and a credit score?

Back to that report card analogy again. So, if we say your credit score is like your final grade, your credit report is your tests, papers, and quizzes that were all averaged to get that grade. Your credit report covers all of the factors that add up to determine your credit score.

In 2004, The Consumer Federation of America polled more than 1,000 Americans and discovered that only one third of those actually understood that their credit score is an assessment of risk. A low credit score means you are a risky bet, a high credit score means you are a safe bet. Which one do you think creditors, lenders, employers, utility companies, and insurers will trust?

Pop Quiz!

Q: How many free credit reports are you annually entitled to under the Fair and Accurate Credit Transactions Act?

A: One from each of the Big Three reporting firms, but you can request as many as you like throughout the year for a small fee.

You may have heard that checking too often on your credit report can actually reduce your score. The truth? The credit reporting software looks for frequent Creditor checks to your report, and if it sees them, it will recognize that you are applying for multiple credit lines at the same time—a potential sign that you could be in financial trouble. However, **if you wish to check on your report yourself, it will have no effect on your score.**

Is my credit report accurate?

A recent study done by the National Association of State Public Interest Research Groups, and reported by CBS found that a shocking 79% of credit reports contain some form of error. It may be small, but any error is unfair and should be corrected.

The information on your credit report is not set in stone. If you find any sort of error, you have the right to have it removed. In fact, under the aptly named Fair and Accurate Credit Report Act of 2004, you have the right to have any negative item removed from your report if it is not 100% accurate OR if it cannot be verified within 30 days. So if you see something you don't like, dispute it with the credit-reporting agency. It's your right.

Understanding Credit Scores: The Final Exam

Now that you have read this mini-tutorial on Credit Scores (and hopefully passed the pop quizzes), it's time for the Final Exam. Pencils ready?

True or False

A credit score of under 600 is good.	True False	**False.** Anything hovering near or below a 600 can cost you thousands of dollars in high interest rates.
Your credit score is available only to banks and lenders.	True False	**False.** Employers, landlords, and even utility companies can evaluate your credit score.
Your credit score is not set in stone.	True False	**True.** Your credit score changes depending on your financial behavior.
If you have a bad credit score, you will never be able to get it high enough to help you get lower interest rates.	True False	**False.** You can improve your credit score by paying bills on time and paying off all debts.
Your credit score is 100% accurate.	True False	**False.** 79% of reports contain small errors that could affect your overall score.
Your credit score has a major effect on your mortgage or interest rates.	True False	**True.** Lenders use your credit score to assess your fiscal responsibility.

Multiple Choice

1) How can you improve your credit score?
    a. Keep debts low.
    b. Pay bills on time.
    c. Establish a long, stable credit history.
    d. All of the above.
Answer: d. Doing all of these things will help improve your score.

2) Choose the best credit score.
    a. 600
    b. 650
    c. 330
    d. 720
Answer: d. The higher the score, the better.

3) Who calculates your credit score?
    a. A credit-reporting agency.
    b. Your bank.
    c. Your accountant.
    d. Anyone who runs a background check on your credit history.
Answer: a. Credit reporting companies collect items on your credit report and compare your behavior to the statistics of similar individuals, granting points for various factors. The sum of those points is your credit score.

4) Why is knowing your credit score important?
    a. It can affect your interest and mortgage rates.
    b. It tells you how much money you have.
    c. It ranks you in order of wealth. Bill Gates has the highest credit score.
    d. You don't need to know; only banks and lenders care about that.
Answer: a. A low credit score can mean high interest and mortgage rates.

Grade Yourself.

How well did you do? If you get an A on your Final Exam, you are one step closer to getting a credit score that is an A on your credit report!

Next, you will learn how to use your credit cards wisely, helping to keep that all-important credit score high and your interest rates low.

PROPER USE
OF CREDIT

DON'T BE "ARMED AND DANGEROUS"

The modern credit card was born in 1951, when the Diners Club issued cards to 200 clients, who could use those cards to purchase meals "on credit" at 27 different NYC restaurants. Since then credit cards have become a standard wallet accessory. But those colorful little plastic cards aren't fashion statements or toys. They pack a powerful punch, so you'd best be careful when handling them.

Fantastic Plastic: The Benefits of Credit Cards

There's no question why credit cards are so popular. Consider the benefits:

- They're convenient
- You can buy now, pay later
- There's no need to carry cash
- You have low minimum monthly payments
- They're handy in emergencies
- They help establish credit
- You can track your spending

But also consider what makes credit cards a bit dangerous:

- They're convenient
- You can buy now, pay later
- You have low minimum monthly payments
- There's no need to carry cash

Whoa, the pros and the cons are almost exactly the same! Yes, the same benefits that make credit cards so popular are the same reasons you have to handle them with care. Here's how.

Plastic Scholastic: Credit Cards Basics

What exactly is a credit card, and how does it work?

When you sign up for an account with a credit card agency, you make an agreement with them promising that if they, in a way, "front" you whatever money you spend under their name (by using their card), you will eventually pay them back, plus some interest, depending on how long it takes you. Now, this little deal is quite handy, but also a big responsibility. Though it may not look like money, feel like money, or even smell like money, a credit card works like real money so it IS real money. The bottom line is: never spend more than you can afford to pay off when the next bill comes. Seems simple enough, right?

How do I get a credit card?

To qualify for a credit card, you must be at least 18 years of age, have a steady source of income, and have a good credit rating. Of course, if you are young or never had a credit card before, you may not have a high credit rating. You will still be able to apply for a credit card, though you may have to pay higher interest rates and have a lower limit than someone with a better credit history. However, by using your new credit card wisely, it will help you establish a good credit history, which will benefit you for the rest of your life.

There are credit card commercials all over TV, and you get tons of "You're Already Approved!" offers in the mail. The first step to using credit cards wisely is to choose the right one for you. With so many credit cards out there, it may seem like an overwhelming task, and unfortunately, there is no simple answer. You have to do a little work to choose the right credit card for you.

To choose the credit card that is best for you, you have to read through the fine print to get down to the nitty-gritty. Choosing a credit card should be taken as seriously as choosing a new car.

How many credit cards do I need?

Don't apply for every credit card offer that comes in the mail, claiming you are "preapproved." It's tricky to juggle several credit card accounts at once, and even a little debt on each one will add up overall. Also, each time a creditor reviews your credit report, it is noted, and if you have tons of available credit it might actually look bad to a potential lender who may wonder how wisely you will use that credit and how likely you will be to repay your loan.

So, select one, two, or three credit cards that you know you will be able to maintain. You can use each card differently: One for regular payments such as rent and utilities, one for luxuries such as dining out or going to the movies, and one for emergencies, such as a burst water pipe or a car accident.

Regarding the card or cards you use regularly, I remind you: Never spend more than you can pay off in the very next statement.

(Remember the Golden Rule of Credit Card Use.) If your balance piles up, interest rates will cost you.

What do I consider when applying for a credit card?

Credit card advertisements promise you a lot. Every one of them boasts great terms, but you have to read the fine print to find the one that is truly best for you.

1. No Annual Fee

Some credit card companies charge a "membership" fee to use their service, but these days, many of them have waived that fee to attract customers. Why pay for something you can get for free?

2. Grace Period

Most credit card companies give you a "grace period," a period of time during which you incur no finance charges. You should always try to pay your balance (in full) during that grace period. Once the due date passes and the grace period ends, you begin incurring late fees. Cards that do not offer you a grace period actually begin charging you interest the instant you make a purchase.

3. Late Fees

Even if you are the most careful credit card user, there may be a month when you are a little late making your payment. When applying for a card, look for one with reasonable late fees.

4. Low Interest Rate

Many credit cards entice you with a low introductory interest rate. But beware, low introductory rates can skyrocket after just a few months. You want to look past the introductory interest rate to the Annual Percentage Rate (APR). Know that the average interest rate is greater than 15%. Even if they advertise that a low rate is permanent, look for high "default rates." If your payment is even an hour late, you could lose your introductory rate forever in favor of a 20% plus "default interest" rate. Finding the lowest APR possible can save you money on the months you have an outstanding balance.

APR What?

The first time I ever applied for a credit card, I asked the customer service lady on the other line to explain to me what APR was and how it affected my statements each month. She couldn't do it. She could tell me that a higher APR was worse . . . but beyond that, she was stumped. The fact is, a lot of us can't explain exactly how APR affects our statements. And it's embarrassing, because it's such a large part of our daily financial life.

APR stands for Annual Percentage Rate, which means it's the amount of interest you pay on your credit card balance yearly. But how can you be paying interest yearly if you pay your credit card monthly and the balance is always changing? It's actually pretty simple. You pay interest on the balance that you don't pay off at the end of the month. To find out how much you pay each month, you multiply the total balance you didn't pay off by the APR and divide by twelve. That'll give you how much you pay in interest per month. it's easier to look at an example.

APR Example

Before Joe Average started playing Reality Millionaire, he didn't know about the Golden Rule of Credit Card Use. So, he used to carry a balance. In the month of January, he carried a $1000 balance on his Visa. His APR on the VISA was 20%. So, to figure out how much he paid in interest that month, he would do the following calculation:

Annual Interest Payment = $1000 X 20% = $200
Interest Payment that Month = $200/12 = $16.67

In this example, Joe pays $16.67 per month to carry the $1,000 balance. It may not seem like much. But it sure as heck adds up.

Plastic Enthusiastic: Credit Card "Goodies"

These days, credit card companies are going above and beyond to get your business. Now many of them are offering rewards programs. Though it may be tempting to sign up for a card that promises you cash back or a free motorcycle, don't get too excited about the treats and forget to check the fine print. All the same rules apply, even when there's 3,000 frequent flyer miles dangling in front of you. You still have to choose the card with the best overall terms.

But what about those rewards? Are they for real?

Many credit card rewards work on a point system. Each time you use your credit card to make a purchase, you earn a certain amount of points toward a reward. Some cards give you free frequent flyer miles or cash back instead of points.

Don't be tempted to overuse your credit card trying to rack up enough points to earn a free mountain bike or enough flyer miles to jet off to Hawaii. You will just wind up running up a huge bill. In the end, that "free" mountain bike could cost you 5 times as much as it's worth.

So, are credit cards rewards a BAD idea?

Consider rewards to be treats, bonuses, or goodies instead of the end goal. Use your credit card as you normally would, and enjoy the bonuses that eventually come your way. You will have earned them by using your card wisely, not by spending more than the free gift is worth in order to win it.

Elastic Plastic: Don't Stretch Yourself Too Thin

If you're not careful, you can make some very large mistakes with credit cards. Particularly if you have a high limit, you can easily wind up spending way more than you can afford. It's easy to whip out that credit card every time you make a purchase, but unfortunately it is also easy to forget that buying something on credit is still spending money.

Always be sure to spend only what you can pay off each month. See a recurring theme here?

What sort of trouble could I get into?

Consider if you run up a balance of $1,000 dollars on your credit card. If your interest rate is the average 15%, and you pay only the minimum payment each month, it could take you over 10 years to pay off your balance. Worse yet, thanks to interest, you will wind up paying $1,758 when you only borrowed $1,000.

Even if you could only afford to pay double the current minimum payment each month, (about $50 each month until debt free) it would take only 2 years and you'd pay $1,157.

Actual Cost Versus Perceived Cost

So in the light of this information, always calculate the ACTUAL cost of a big-ticket item, such as a new TV or expensive purse. If you consider your current balance, what you will be able to pay each month, and interest rates, the price tag could add up to a price that simply isn't worth it.

Drastic Plastic: What To Do If You Get Into Debt

If you do find yourself in the hole, don't panic. You can work yourself out of it.

Transfer Your Balance

Transfer all your outstanding balances to the card with the lowest interest rate.

Negotiate For a Lower Rate

If you have been a good customer with a good credit history, your credit card company will not want to lose you. In fact, they WANT you to take a long time to pay off your balance because they earn more money the longer it takes you.

Call them up and ask for a lowered interest rate. You may even threaten to cancel your account with them and move to a competitor. You'd be surprised by what credit card companies will do to keep you as a client.

Remove Temptation

If you find you aren't that responsible with credit, take your card OUT OF YOUR WALLET and keep it in a safe place. Do not be tempted to use it. You cannot afford to drive up any more debt. Do not adopt the "I am already in debt, what's a little more?" mentality.

Pay, Pay, Pay

Follow the rules from Round Three and pay diligently each month. If it means putting yourself on a budget and giving up a few small luxuries, do it. You wouldn't pay $20 for a $5 cup of coffee, would you? But that's what happens if you keep living in debt.

Don't Be Discouraged

When you are in debt, life may seem like an uphill battle. But remember, take baby steps. Every little bit helps.

Plastic Bombastic: Avoiding Credit Card Fraud

The bad guys are pretty darn gutsy these days. Criminals have no qualms about lifting your credit card number at any opportunity, then waltzing around using your credit to buy all sorts of expensive items. What's worse then being in debt? Being in somebody else's debt.

Identity thieves are tricky, pompous, and extremely daring. Here are some simple steps to avoid seeing strange and scary charges wind up on your credit card bill.

• Always sign new cards right away.

- Cut old cards into many pieces, and throw the bits away in different receptacles.

- Also shred (or burn) old receipts or anything with your credit card number on it. Throw it all away in different receptacles. That way nobody can sift through your trash to put together your account number.

- Never fax your credit card number to anyone—who knows how many people could see it before it gets in the right hands.

- Only give out your account number over the phone or the Internet if YOU initiate the transaction, not if someone calls out of the blue and asks for it.

- When making purchases on the Internet, make absolutely sure you are logged onto a secure connection. Secure servers begin with "https://" rather than the usual connection "http://." Also look for a small padlock symbol in the bottom or top right-hand corner of your screen. These are indicators that the site has made an effort to protect your credit card information.

- Report any signs of trouble immediately. Credit card companies have 24-hour support lines, so you can cancel a stolen card instantly without losing precious hours (and dollars) when a card is being used fraudulently.

What do I do if I see suspicious charges on my bill?

Always, always, always go over your monthly credit card statement with a fine-tooth comb. You can catch any charges you didn't make or charges that you may be disputing with a merchant. Watch that any returned items were properly credited to your account.

You have 60 days from when you receive your bill to dispute any of the charges. Contact the credit card company, as well as the merchant, with your name, address, phone number, and order or invoice number. You are entitled to a response within 30 days, and all issues must be resolved within two billing cycles.

Now, remember, even if you are involved in a dispute; don't forget to pay the rest of the money you owe. In the event of a dispute, you may also request an extension on your credit line. Sometimes, if you have good credit history, the extension is automatically granted.

No More Words Rhyme With Plastic: At Least None That Would Make Sense

Handling a credit card account is a big responsibility. But if you follow one basic rule, you will be able to keep control of your spending and enjoy all of the benefits of a credit card account without any of the negatives. That rule? I said it before; I'll say it again:

Never spend more than you can pay off in full on the next credit card bill.

There's a reason that the chapter on credit cards is the last chapter in Reality Millionaire. Credit cards are the number one reason Americans get into so much trouble with debt. In just a little over 50 years, credit cards have changed the way we do our day-to-day finances. Sadly, for the most part, the change hasn't been good. Credit cards encourage us to live outside our means—and that means getting in over our heads.

We can't get ahead if we're always trying to catch up. We can't get wealthy, if we're drowning in monthly debt payments. But now you know how to get away from debt, treat credit cards wisely, get back to the starting line, run the race and burst through to the finish line.

So that's it. You've now officially had Finance 101. You have all the tools you need to go forth and pursue your financial dreams be that comfort, travel, retirement, hobbies, education—or just getting filthy rich!

APPENDIX A

INVESTMENT TYPES

A cash investment is a highly liquid investment that can easily be converted to cash. Money market accounts, CDs, and even your savings account are considered cash investments.

Money Market Accounts

 A money market account is a Federal Deposit Insurance Corporation (FDIC)–insured account that earns higher interest than a basic savings account. Putting some of your earnings into a money market account is similar to placing it into a savings account at the bank, but the rules are a little different. While the bank pools all its money together to conduct cash transactions for thousands of people, the cash from a money

market account is pooled a bit differently—it goes into the money market, not the bank vault, where it is combined with other cash investments that get recycled into the money market. Because the money has to remain in the money market to maintain high liquidity, withdrawals and check writing are typically limited for money market account holders. The benefit is the higher interest earned on your account for a relatively short period of time.

But what exactly is the money market? Much like the Internet, the money market doesn't exist in a physical space—it works on the premise of liquid assets being bought, sold and traded. It is most closely associated with New York City, our financial capital, also home to the stock exchange. Like stocks, bonds and mutual funds are the physical assets traded on the stock exchange, cash and short-term government bonds are the physical assets traded on the money market.

Still difficult to get your mind around? The money market is home for highly liquid assets, such as cash. Liquidity is the degree to which an asset can change hands without losing value. To better understand liquidity, think of it this way: imagine cars on a freeway loop with several entrance and exit ramps. The traffic on the loop, constantly flowing in a circle, represents the flow of cash inside the money market. The entrance and exit ramps connote points where cash comes and goes with trading—buying and selling. As long as cars continue to enter, drive around and exit the loop, the traffic flows. So it is with the money market—it thrives on the circulation of our most liquid assets, notably cash.

You might be wondering what this has to do with your money. When you invest in a money market account, your dollars earn much higher interest than they would in a regular savings or passbook account. That is, a money market account will give you (as the old expression goes) more bang for your buck.

There are a few drawbacks to money market accounts; while they earn higher interest than a savings account, they also impose certain limitations. For starters, you must invest and maintain a minimum balance—fees may be imposed if the minimum balance is not kept. There's also usually a limit on check writing. Unlike your typical checking account, a money market account does not typically allow unlimited check writing. Service fees may be applied as penalties for over-writing checks or failing to maintain your balance.

Money Market Account Highlights

Definition: A high-interest, limited savings account.

Where to Get It: Any FDIC-insured financial institution, Federal Reserve Banks.

Pros:
- FDIC insured
- Keeps money liquid and accessible, as opposed to stocks
- Earns higher interest than a traditional savings or checking account

Cons:
- May require a minimum balance
- Imposes limitations on check writing
- Can incorporate maintenance fees

CDs

The Average Joe probably owns dozens of CDs, but they're not making him any money. That is, his compact discs. In the finance world, CDs have nothing to do with listening to The Beatles or Beethoven's Ninth—they are a means of saving money in an interest-earning account.

CD stands for "Certificate of Deposit," a promissory note issued to you by a bank, ensuring that the sum you wish to deposit and hold in an account will earn interest at a specific rate and time period. CDs can be purchased in any denomination. As the CD matures, the interest you earn will go directly into your CD savings account.

There are over 250 different types of CDs, ranging from simple one month or one year savings accounts to more extensive, long-term CDs that can be applied to special accounts, such as IRAs.

As with many investments, you will be charged a fee for any withdrawals made from a CD before its maturity date. This is an important consideration for you as an investor when deciding on the longevity of the CD you plan to purchase.

While CDs are safe, stable investments, they have comparatively low interest rates and annual yields. Thus, they tend to be more beneficial as short-term investments.

CD Highlights

Definition: An interest-earning savings account issued by a commercial bank, with a fixed maturity date.

Where to Get It: Any commercial, FDIC-insured bank.

Pros:
• Very safe investment
• Diverse longevity, one month and up
• Available in any sum
• Convenient to purchase

Cons:
• Low interest and return rates
• Penalties for early withdrawal

FIXED INCOME

Fixed income investments are modes of investments that pay fixed interest or payments over a set period of time. When they are purchased, they are purchased with fixed maturity dates and interest rates, so that you know exactly what you will be earning over the life of the investment.

Bonds

You know that debt is bad for you, but what about becoming a creditor yourself? That's what bonds are all about. Bonds are actually forms of debt. That is to say, bonds indebt certain entities to you. When you purchase bonds, you become the First Bank of John Doe, loaning your money out for a specific period of time over which you will be paid interest and eventually have your principal investment returned.

Bonds can be issued by governments or corporations. The government or the corporation, known as the issuer, borrows against your investment and pays you interest based on a fixed rate, known as a coupon.

Treasury Bonds

Treasury bonds are a way for Uncle Sam to use your money and pay you back with interest. Treasury bonds are government bonds, available for purchase directly from the U.S. Treasury through the aptly named program, Treasury Direct. You can visit their website at www.treasurydirect.gov. Although there are many different bond issuers to choose from, government bonds are considered among the most secure.

There are three main types of Government Treasury bonds:

1) **Treasury bonds, which mature at 10 years or more;**
2) **Treasury notes, which mature between 1 and 5 years;**
3) **Treasury bills ("T-bills"), which mature in one year or less.**

The maturity date is the date at which the principal is to be paid back to you by the issuer, in this case, the U.S. government. This interest rate, known as a coupon, is predetermined by the particular sort of bond purchased, as is the schedule on which it is paid. Most interest is paid semiannually.

Treasury Bond Highlights

Definition: A loan to the government in a particular amount, on which interest is earned up to the date of maturity, when the principal is repaid plus interest earned.

Where to Get It: A bond brokerage (beware of minimum investments), some banks, or Treasury Direct.

Pros:
- Low-risk, stable investment
- Diverse maturity dates, ranging from one month to 10+ years
- Fixed-income security—you know exactly what you're due and when

Cons:
- May not earn as much as a stock investment
- May require minimum purchase of $5,000 or more

Corporate Bonds

A corporate bond is a bond issued by (you guessed it) a corporation. Corporate bonds have potentially the highest yields of any type of bond investment. As you may know already, a higher return usually equals a higher level of risk, and that equation holds true of corporate bonds.

As with any investment, it's really important to do your homework before purchasing and investing in a corporate bond. You'd want to know the credit risk associated with investing in a corporation before you give them your money, right? Of course. You wouldn't loan a friend $100 if he'd never paid back a debt in his life—and the same idea applies to purchasing corporate bonds. Knowing that a company has paid off its debt and is making a profit is an important factor in your decision to invest in their bonds.

Most corporate bonds are known as debentures, meaning that they are not secured with any kind of collateral. So, if the company goes bust—so do you. This risk is why it's so important to investigate corporate financial histories before investing.

The flip side of the situation, however, is that corporate bonds will almost always produce a higher yield than government bonds. Your job is to calculate the risk of the investment before entering into it.

Corporate Bond Highlights

Definition: A security purchased by you as a loan to a corporation, who pays interest on the loan until it matures.

Where to Get It: Brokerages

Pros:
- High yield
- Regular coupon payments
- Can go up in value over time

Cons:
- Higher level of risk (than other bonds)
- Can be "called" by corporation (purchased back)
- Investment can be lost entirely upon corporate default

EQUITY

An equity investment is one in which the shares you purchase determine your level of ownership of the entity offering the shares. In other words, if you purchase a piece of equity, you own that piece. If you buy 5% of a company's stock, you technically own 5% of the company.

Stocks

We all know that rich guys own stock. The average Joe, however, may not know much about what stock is, or how it's traded. One can't rely on tips you hear from friends on your coffee break— remember the "dotcom" bust? The worst mistakes in dealing with

MIKE PETERSON

stock are made by people who think they can make a fast dollar in an investment that takes decades to pay off.

A piece of stock, or share, is a piece of equity, i.e., ownership in a company. If you buy shares of stock in Coca-Cola or Uncle Joe's Soda Co., you actually own a percentage of its business. If Uncle Joe's has 1,000 shares of stock, and you buy 100, you technically own 10% of his business.

But what does ownership mean? It certainly doesn't entitle you to a lifetime of free soda. Typically, one share equals one vote towards electing the company's board of directors. And unfortunately, the reality of that vote is even less exciting than it sounds. The real benefit and beauty of investing in stock isn't the ownership—it's the payoff, in the form of both dividends and capital gain.

Stock dividends are, for all intents and purposes, chunks of free money. They are the earned income of your shares over time and the products of the company's profit. If your stock investments pay you dividends, you will earn more money as the company continues to perform well financially.

But dividends aren't the only way stocks pay off. Capital gain is what happens to an asset when it is sold at a higher value than its purchase price. It occurs at the point of sale, so even if you don't get dividends, buying and selling stock as its value increases is another profitable way to play the stock market.

There is a lot of risk involved in stock investments—do you want the good news or the bad news first? The bad news is, your entire investment depends upon the financial success of the company in which you've invested—if it flops, you won't be able to resell your shares. Ever. So, you will have lost any money you invested in them. The good news is the flip side of that same coin; not only can you make tremendous profits off of successful businesses, but even if you lose, you cannot be stripped of your part ownership of the company. Even if Uncle Joe's goes bankrupt and is liquidated, you will be paid your percentage of what's left after his debts are collected.

Risk is part of the whole stock market game. To some, it's exciting—to others, frightening. But the truth is, stocks have consistently made people more money than any other type of investment since the market's inception, and they are a standard part of any well-rounded portfolio.

Common Stock

There are two general types of stock: common and preferred. Common stock is the most typical class of stock, and also carries the most risk. Just as described above, common stock shares are equivalent to one vote per share to elect the company's board of directors, and also represent a particular claim on that company's profits (a.k.a., dividends). Common stock typically has a higher yield than any other class of shares because of its high-risk level.

Preferred Stock

"Preferred stock" has an odd name because it typically isn't actually preferred over the "common" stock, and is similar in nature to bonds. When you purchase preferred stock, you may forfeit your voting right in exchange for fixed and guaranteed dividends—not a bad deal, especially since individual stock owners have very little influence when it comes to corporate management. A potential drawback of preferred stock, however, is its vulnerability as your asset. Many companies reserve the right to purchase back preferred stock at any time, which would leave you without future dividends.

Stocks Highlights

Definition: Equity, or part ownership of a company and its profits.
Where to Get It: Brokerages

Pros:
- Can yield higher returns than any other investment
- Tends to be stable over an extended period of time, as in decades
- Diversifies your portfolio

Cons:
- High level of risk
- Can be unstable in the short term

MIXED INVESTMENTS

A mixed investment allows you to invest in a variety of assets all at once—stocks, government bonds, corporate bonds, and even liquid cash.

Mutual Funds

A mutual fund is a popular type of mixed investment that allows you to earn money over the long term by investing in a collection of securities. Imagine a big club sandwich—turkey, bacon, lettuce, tomato, and cheese, all held together by slices of bread. This image is a helpful way to understand the mutual fund. All of the different ingredients represent different types of stocks and bonds, and the bread that holds them all together is the fund itself.

Simply put, a mutual fund is a collection of stocks, bonds and sometimes cash investments. Your money is invested, in small increments, into a large, diverse group of investments. The way you earn money through a mutual fund is by an amalgamation of the dividends you receive from the stocks, the capital gains in the price per share for the mutual fund, and the interest you earn on the bonds.

One of the advantages of purchasing a mutual fund is that it allows a lot of people to pool their funds to purchase a variety of stocks, bonds and cash that would have been inconvenient or expensive to purchase separately. Also, a fund manager is in charge of purchasing the individual investments for the fund, so the investors don't have to worry about picking their own stocks and bonds. Having a professional manage the fund is less risky than doing it yourself (at least theoretically). Hence, mutual funds are favored by people who want to earn a return on their investments without playing hardball in the stock market or risk poorly managing their investments.

The other big advantage to owning a mutual fund is diversification. If you took $10 and used it to buy a few slices of turkey, a slab of bacon, a piece of cheese, a tomato, and a head of lettuce, two dollars went into each part of the sandwich. Similarly, if you invested $100 into a mutual fund, a few dollars would purchase a portion of each investment in the group. This instant diversification helps shield you from hinging your financial future to the ups and downs of a single stock or bond.

There are several ways in which you can earn a return on your investment in a mutual fund:

- *Dividends and Interest.* As we already discussed, if your fund is diversified, or divided into investments into both stocks and bonds. Therefore, you will then earn dividends (profit) from the stocks, and interest from the bonds or cash investments.

- *Capital Gain.* If your mutual fund increases in value before you sell it, you will have earned a capital gain. Or, if the value increases while you own it and you decide to sell it, you will get more money per share than you paid for it. Therefore, you've made a profit through capital gain, but that profit is taxable. Heard of the Capital Gains Tax? This tax will apply to you if you purchase or sell assets whose value has increased.

- *Simple Profit.* If your investments increase in price, they can be sold by your investment manager for a profit.

Your earnings from the mutual fund you choose will either be reinvested into more securities, or given to you by check, depending upon your preference.

Mutual Fund Highlights

Definition: A diversified investment in securities, including shares of stocks, bond, cash investments, or some combination of the three.

Where to Get It: Mutual fund companies, brokerages.

Pros:
- Managed by a finance professional
- Lower risk investment if properly diversified
- High liquidity—earnings can usually be converted easily into cash
- Can be extremely diversified—much more so than purchasing a single stock

Cons:
- Dependence on fund manager for investment decisions
- Dilution of funds from overdiversification
- Lower risk can mean lower returns

RETIREMENT ACCOUNTS

A retirement account is an investment for the future. Typically, it will have limited withdrawal privileges, since the goal is to save over the long term. Retirement accounts are often offered by workplaces to their employees, but they may also be purchased by individuals.

401(k)

A 401(k) plan is a kind of retirement account offered by many U.S. companies. If your employer offers a 401(k) plan, this is often one of the best ways to secure your retirement, especially if your employer matches a portion of your contribution. However, as was brought sharply to the nation's attention with the fall of Enron in 2001, you should watch carefully what kinds of investments your company has available with their 401(k) plan. The investments put into your retirement account can be stocks, bonds, mutual funds, or other investment types of varying risk. Just because it's a 401(k) doesn't necessarily mean "without risk."

The 401(k) gets its name from the section of the IRS document that defines it. It has become a generic term for an interest-earning retirement plan offered by a private company to its employees that follows specific guidelines. Cash invested into a 401(k) program is tax-deferred, meaning you won't have to pay taxes on the money until you withdraw it. In fact, making an early withdrawal will earn you a slap on the wrist from the federal government in the form of financial penalty (10% on top of regular income tax), so your best advice is to leave it alone until it matures. After all, 401(k)s are supposed to help you find the money to retire on a yacht in Majorca, not pay for a family vacation to Spain this spring.

Apart from the general guidelines and occasional censure for early withdrawal, 401(k) programs are not government insured or regulated. Most employers opt for a third party managed 401(k) plan that contains several options for the employee to choose from—the company does not typically determine how the money will be invested.

I should also mention that investing through a 401(k), or a standard IRA, will reduce your taxable income by the amount invested in that year. For example: If I make $30,000 this year, but invest $3,000 in a 401(k) or a Traditional IRA, my taxable income for the state and the federal governments will be only $27,000.

Despite the small risk, most company plans are responsible, and a good 401(k) plan is invaluable to your investment portfolio and your retirement future. If your employer is matching part of your contributions, not investing in your company's 401(k) plan is like throwing money down the drain.

Example: Joe Average's employer offers him a 50% matching contribution on the money he puts into the company 401(k), which typically earns around 8% interest. If Joe uses the extra $370 he found from Round Two and invests in his 401(k), at the end of 10 years Joe will have almost $114,000 in his 401(k). Over those ten years he contributed only a little over $44,000. The rest of the almost $70,000 is earned from interest and employer contributions.

JOE AVERAGE'S 401(k) PLAN ACCOUNT VALUE AFTER 10 YEARS

Year	Joe's Contribution	Employer Matching 50% Contribution	Total Account Value
1	4,440.00	2,220.00	6,973.88
2	4,440.00	2,220.00	14,678.03
3	4,440.00	2,220.00	23,188.90
4	4,440.00	2,220.00	32,590.97
5	4,440.00	2,220.00	42,977.56
10	4,440.00	2,220.00	113,688.95

But do all 401(k) plans perform so well? How do you know if your 401(k) plan is a good one? A strong 401(k) plan is diversified. Even better, a strong 401(k) plan gives you control over the plan's investments and lets you customize your investments based on your risk tolerance, age and retirement goals

401(k) Highlights

Definition: A tax-deferred employee retirement plan that meets IRS regulations for 401(k) plans, often featuring employer-match contributions.

Where to Get It: Your employer.

Pros:

- Employer matching contributions can make them one of your highest returning investment options for the amount of risk involved.
- They are easy to enroll in and offered directly at your workplace.
- Contributions can often be deducted directly from your paycheck, so you don't miss the money.
- Strong 401(k) plans will allow a healthy diversification of investments and customization of those investments to your needs—all in one place without having to visit multiple firms or brokers.
- Earnings and investments are tax-deferred, meaning you don't have to pay taxes until you take the money out.

Cons:

- The access to your money is limited. 401(k)s are retirement plans, and you pay a penalty for early withdrawal, although there are some instances in which you can take a loan from yourself for certain life events such as the purchase of your first home (not recommended).
- If the 401(k) offered at your company invests heavily in company stock as its only plan option, you may end up without a job and without an investment fund if your company has a bad year.

IRAs and Roth IRAs

If you've ever talked to your friends about their IRAs, you probably understand an IRA to be a type of investment. Actually, they aren't investments at all. IRA stands for "Individual Retirement Account," a very, very useful kind of account that can save you hundreds of thousands of dollars by retirement.

It's easiest to think of an IRA as money that the IRS treats differently than other money. As of 2007, the IRS has mandated that you can allocate up to $4,000 per year to an IRA. You can use that money to invest in a variety of things: CDs, stocks, bonds, etc. But, what makes an IRA so special is that this IRA investment money accrues interest that is tax-deferred or tax-exempt (depending on what kind of account you have). How often do you get to hear the words "tax-exempt" in your financial life?

Like the 401(k), this account is intended as a retirement fund, but unlike the 401(k), the IRA is managed by the individual and not by an employer or company. In short, the IRS has decided to give you a tax break if you're saving for retirement.

There are two primary kinds of IRAs, Roth and Traditional. A Roth IRA offers tax-free earnings. A traditional IRA is a tax-deferred account.

Roth IRA. If you choose to have a Roth IRA, your growth and interest will be tax-exempt, meaning that you pay taxes as usual on the amount you put into the account. However, all earnings generated over the lifetime of the account are tax-free and will never be taxed, even when you withdraw them. In order to qualify to fully fund a Roth IRA, however, your adjusted gross income (AGI) must be less than:

• $150,000 if married and filing jointly
• $95,000 if single/head of household
• $10,000 if married filing separately

Traditional IRA. A regular IRA is tax-deferred, meaning you can put funds into the IRA account up until the 15th of April of the following year—and still claim the deduction. Also, you don't have to pay tax on the interest accumulated, as long as it stays in the account. You must, however, pay taxes on both the principal and the earned interest when you withdraw it for retirement.

As with most things in life, you can't have your cake and eat it, too— you have to choose which IRA is best for you. So, which one is better? The answer is easy. If you plan to be in a lower tax bracket at retirement time, then you save more money with the regular IRA. If you think you'll be in a higher tax bracket, it's better to bite the bullet and pay the taxes now with the Roth IRA, provided you qualify.

But what do you buy with your IRA money? The money can be used to purchase any number of investments—stocks, bonds, mutual funds, CDs—any sort of investment you feel is most appropriate for accomplishing your future financial goals. You are free to buy and sell any asset within your IRA as long as you don't take any of the money you earn out of the account. Remember, the money is for retirement, so just like a 401(k), you'll be penalized for early withdrawal.

Example: Joe Average puts the maximum amount into his Roth IRA account every year. In 35 years, he will have saved almost $1,500,000 if he got a 10% rate of return. During that time he will have only contributed about $188,000. The other $1,312,000 of that is free money! He doesn't even have to pay taxes on it, as long as it is a Roth IRA (if it's a Traditional IRA, he will have to pay tax as he withdraws the money).

IRA Highlights

IRA Definition: IRA stands for Individual Retirement Account and is one of the simplest kinds of retirement accounts defined by the IRS.

Where to Get It? Mutual fund companies, banks, brokerages.

Pros:
- Depending on the type, IRAs are either tax-deferred or tax-exempt
- Penalties for withdrawal ensure steady savings
- Easy to purchase

Cons:
- Early withdrawal penalties apply
- Deposits are limited yearly

APPENDIX B

VOCABULARY

12b-1 Fee—fee exacted to cover marketing expenses of the mutual fund provider; allows mutual fund provider to use mutual fund assets to cover its business expenses.

401(k)—plan offered by employers to allow their employees to accrue retirement savings by placing a portion of their salaries into a diversified investment plan.

ADV Form—document retained in the Securities & Exchange Commission's records containing relevant information regarding a registered investment advisor.

appreciation—the increase in value of an asset.

asset—an entity of economic or financial value, owned by an individual or a corporation, that is expected to increase in value over time.

back-end load—sales charge on mutual fund exacted when money is withdrawn.

benchmark—a standard by which a security's performance can be measured.

bond—certificate issued by a company or the government promising payment of interest on an investor's loan for a given period of time.

brokerage—an institution offering financial services regarding the planning, trading, and selling of investments by brokers. See discount brokerage and full service brokerage.

broker—an individual responsible for buying and selling investments and securities and sometimes giving financial advice.

capital gain—an increase in the value of an asset that is realized at the point of its sale and must be claimed on taxes by the seller.

cash asset—asset which can be converted to legal tender at any time.

CD (Certificate of Deposit)—promissory note issued by a bank allowing the bearer to receive interest on a sum of money.

CFP® (Certified Financial Planner™)—a professional who has been certified to give competent and ethical financial planning advice by the Certified Financial Planner Board of Standards.

commission-based planning—refers to when a financial planner earns his/her income when you implement their suggested plan; commissions are earned on securities you purchase through him/her.

common stock—shares of equity (ownership in a company) that carry the privilege of one vote per share for the board of directors of a corporation.

compounded interest—interest applied to the principal and interest combined; interest that earns interest on top of itself.

coupon—predetermined interest rate from a bond issuer.

creditor—entity to which debt is owed.

debenture—an unsecured debt.

debtor—individual who has retained debt, i.e., anyone who pays a mortgage, uses credit cards, or has taken out a loan.

discount brokerage—a discount brokerage charges a nominal, commission-based fee for investment services, but does not provide investment advice.

dividend—a payment in the form of cash, stock or properties made to a company's stockholders from its profits.

equity—type of investment which renders you part owner of the entity invested in, such as a stock.

face value—the amount borrowed/loaned on a bond. See principal.

Fair And Accurate Credit Transactions Act—federal law established in 2003 to protect consumers applying for mortgages and other forms of credit; tightened legislation on identity theft and consumer credit information to help prevent abuse of consumer information.

FDCPA (Fair Debt Collection and Practices Act)—federal law that protects debtors from aggressive collectors who engage in unfair practices, such as misrepresentation.

fee-only planning—refers to when a financial planner is paid directly for his/her services.

fixed-income security—investment in which you know at the start exactly how much money will be returned to you, as with a bond.

front-end load—fee exacted from mutual fund when money is deposited.

full service brokerage—brokerage that provides multiple services in addition to investment advice, such as tax and retirement planning, typically for higher, commission-based fees.

index fund—investment portfolio managed in such a way that its growth or deflation mirrors that of the stock market.

inflation—increase in market prices over time.

interest—a charge, usually expressed as a percentage, for the privilege of borrowing money; term can also denote percentage of ownership of a stock.

IRA (Individual Retirement Account)—allows a single individual to invest particular amounts of savings into an account with limited withdrawal ability, designated for retirement (both tax exempt and tax-deductible, see Roth IRA and Traditional IRA).

issuer—the entity, usually the government or a corporation, who sells a bond.

liquidity—the degree to which an asset can be bought, sold, or traded without affecting its value; cash is the most liquid of all assets.

load—one-time sales charge on a mutual fund.

maturity—the date at which a bond must be repaid.

money market account—interest-earning savings account through a secured financial institution; usually earns more than a typical savings account, but limits your transaction capabilities.

mutual fund—investment that spreads money into multiple and or various stocks and bonds, creating lower risk.

portfolio—an investor's collection of assets.

preferred stock—shares in corporate equity with a specific dividend to be paid to investors, who usually do not have voting rights.

principal—original amount invested into an account or borrowed on a loan, exclusive of interest.

return on investment—percentage of loss or gain in a given security over a particular period of time.

risk profile—the allocation of stocks, bonds and cash in an investment portfolio based on the investor's tolerance to risk and the time he/she has until retirement.

Roth IRA—Individual Retirement Account in which you pay regular taxes upon contributing to the account, but earnings within the account and withdrawals from it are tax-free.

ROI—Return on Investment. Refers to the percentage of profit earned from an investment.

S&P—Standard & Poor's, a financial services company that rates the performance of stocks and bonds according to their levels of risk.

S&P 500—collection of 500 companies whose stock is monitored and rated by S&P; reflects the state of "the market" in general.

S&P Index Fund—investment that reflects the growth or deflation of the S&P 500 stocks.

SEC (Securities & Exchange Commission)—an organization created by Congress to protect investors.

security—contract representing ownership of stocks and bonds.

share—a piece of equity that denotes ownership.

simple interest—charge for the privilege of borrowing money from a financial institution, usually expressed as a percentage rate.

stock—a piece of equity, or share, that denotes part ownership of a company's assets and/or earnings.

Social Security—a federal program designed to provide benefits such as retirement pensions and disability income.

tax-exempt—an account in which interest earned within an account is tax-free.

tax-deductible—an account to which contributions can be deducted from the contributor's taxable income.

Traditional IRA—Individual Retirement Account in which contributions are tax-deductible, but taxes are paid on withdrawals from the account.

Treasury bond—U.S. government-issued security with a fixed interest rate that matures after ten years or more.

Treasury note—U.S. government-issued security with a fixed interest rate that matures over a period of one to ten years.

yield—annual rate of return expressed as a percentage; also the amount of money earned from stock investments, or interest earned from bond investments.

INDEX

Notes

Check out our website:
www.realitymillionaire.com
to review:

New self-help financial articles
Financial calculators
Sign up for our newsletter

If you would like a
FREE
workbook that
will help you to:

• **Free up 10%-15%
of your income**

• **Build an
emergency fund**

• **Eliminate debt**

• **Build wealth**

Go to: **www.realitymillionaire.com/booklet**

We will send you the 28 page booklet
"Debt-Free In Record Time" Free of charge.